Confiscation
Gold as Contraband 1933-1975

Kenneth R. Ferguson

Austin, Texas

This first-edition copy is printed in 11-point Garamond.

ISBN: 1981674055
ISBN-13: 978-1981674053

Printed in the United States of America.

ABOUT THE AUTHOR

Kenneth R. Ferguson received his master's degree from the Lyndon B. Johnson School of Public Affairs at the University of Texas at Austin in 1973. He made his living as a professional coin dealer for over 40 years, serving as both President of the Texas Coin Dealers Association and Consultant to the American Numismatic Association. He has lived in Austin since 1966.

CONTENTS

PART II: GOLD AS CONTRABAND

PART III: PROSPECTS FOR GOLD

The power to issue bills and "regulate values" of coin cannot be so enlarged as to authorize arbitrary action, whose immediate purpose and necessary effect is destruction of individual rights.

James C. McReynolds, Supreme Court Justice
The Gold Clause Cases, Dissenting Opinion, 1935

PREFACE

Some political misjudgments of the past are so notorious that today they are referenced by a single word: Prohibition, Appeasement, Internment, Escalation. The confiscation of gold from American residents in 1933 should be included in that category, yet mainstream history books and economic texts give little, if any, coverage to the topic. The bibliography for this work includes many preeminent authors and famous texts, yet only *A Monetary History of the United States 1867-1960* by Friedman and Schwartz provides anything but a cursory discussion of the subject, with some only mentioning the "surrender" of privately held gold and nothing more. The only comprehensive references to this episode in history are in original documents—executive orders, congressional acts, judicial opinions, and recorded speeches—easily available to any persistent internet researcher.

Whether this oversight by historians and economists is intentional or not, political or not, judgmental or not, it needs to be addressed. The academic community, for whatever reason, does not consider the confiscation of gold worthy of intelligent analysis or discussion. This dismissive attitude gives short change to the legitimate concerns of the people who were most opposed to President Roosevelt's gold policies—farmers, blue collar workers, small business proprietors—and who believed democracy had been circumvented.

Just a few years earlier, in the late 1920s, the mere thought of gold confiscation would have been inconceivable to everyone, including those who later supported it. How and why it happened deserves proper examination; it is an essential part of American history.

PART I:

CRISIS AND CONFISCATION

I.

AN ECONOMIC REFERENDUM

On November 8, 1932, Franklin D. Roosevelt was elected President of the United States. He defeated Herbert Hoover, a sitting President running on the Republican ticket for a second term. Roosevelt won by an overwhelming margin, capturing 42 of 48 states, winning the popular vote by over 7 million, and leading the Democratic party to large majorities in both the House and the Senate. The President-elect was given a clear mandate for change, but what form that change would take was as yet uncertain.

The campaign was more conservative than Roosevelt's eventual presidency. The Democratic party platform included a call for a balanced budget and reduced federal expenditures, both bedrock principles of past Republican administrations. Roosevelt separated himself from Hoover by pledging aid to agriculture, new federal works programs, and increased assistance to the poor, but the major political differences between the candidates centered on the Great Depression—who caused it, and what should be done. The Republicans blamed foreign interests and the aftermath of World War I, while the Democrats blamed Hoover and his policies. Roosevelt's advisers believed they could win the election by avoiding major mistakes on the campaign trail and making Hoover's track record the dominant issue. The desperate condition of the American economy turned the election into an economic referendum.

The Great Depression began with the stock market crash of 1929, and by election day it was more than three years old, with no end in sight. Never in American history had an economic downturn been so lengthy and so brutal. From August 1929 to March 1933, the money supply fell more than one third, the number of commercial banks was reduced by over 9,000, the Standard and Poor's stock index fell by 80%, and the unemployment rate rose to 25%. In human terms, the costs were visible everywhere—foreclosures on homes and family farms, people desperate for work, others waiting in bread lines. New York City parks were mockingly called "Hoovervilles" for the tents and makeshift dwellings that provided shelter for the city's homeless.

This was the backdrop to Roosevelt's election. Inauguration was not until March 4, 1933, so the President-elect had 115 days to assemble an entirely new executive branch, including cabinet secretaries and White House officials. He also had to work out the details of his administration's policies and legislative priorities, which had been avoided during the campaign with only the vague promise of a "New Deal," but now required more specificity. Even with these short-term challenges, however, Roosevelt anticipated a smooth transition. As of election day, there was no expectation or fear of an imminent crisis. Nonetheless, events leading up to the oath of office would shock the country, and precipitate an exercise of power unprecedented in peacetime.

THE BANKING CRISIS OF 1933

During his Presidential campaign, Roosevelt rarely, if ever, mentioned the gold standard, or possible devaluation of the dollar—though these topics were of considerable importance among international bankers. Great Britain had abandoned the gold standard in 1931, and within a year, 25 other countries had followed suit. By election day, the only countries still on the gold standard—besides the United States—were France, Belgium, Luxembourg, the Netherlands, Italy, Poland, and Switzerland. The American Treasury and Federal Reserve System owned the largest share of the world's gold supply, but with the domino effect of so many other countries dropping out, central bankers and large private interests in Europe questioned America's ability to continue support for the current gold standard. They began to convert dollar assets into gold in anticipation of a dollar devaluation. The resulting drain of American gold reserves was significant, but not yet critical.

While foreigners doubted our ability to continue support of an official gold price of $20.67 per troy ounce, Americans witnessed the closing of many local banks, and began withdrawing gold and cash, putting great pressure on local bank cash reserves. The Federal Reserve acted quickly to increase the money supply by purchasing outstanding government securities, and the Reconstruction Finance Corporation, established in January 1932, made loans to individual banks in financial trouble. Contemporary wisdom held that the financial difficulties of the depression were both temporary and manageable.

The first hint of crisis occurred eight days before the election. On October 31, in reaction to a wave of bank runs throughout the state, Nevada declared a bank holiday, temporarily suspending all bank obligations and payments. Due to Nevada's sparse population and limited economy, however, its problems were generally discounted as an isolated case.

Ironically, the loans made by the Reconstruction Finance Corporation were indirectly responsible for making matters worse. In January 1933, the House of Representatives passed a resolution requiring the identities of all banks receiving RFC assistance to be published. With their financial condition made public, each of the affected banks suffered an immediate run on their deposits. On January 20, Iowa declared a bank holiday, followed by Louisiana on February 3, and Michigan on February 14. By March 3, the day before inauguration, almost half the states had declared a bank holiday in some form. Gold deposits at the New York Federal Reserve Bank fell below required minimums, as withdrawal demands from at home and abroad continued. President-elect Roosevelt was about to assume leadership of a government that in the previous two weeks had lost all control over its currency.

A NATIONAL BANK HOLIDAY

It only took two days in office for the new president to respond forcefully to the crisis. On March 6, Roosevelt issued a proclamation declaring "emergency executive control over all banking and currency transactions." It read, in part,

> WHEREAS there have been heavy and unwarranted withdrawals of gold and currency from our banking institutions for the purpose of hoarding; and
> WHEREAS continuous and increasingly extensive speculative activity abroad in foreign exchange has resulted in severe drains on the nation's stocks of gold; and
> WHEREAS these conditions have created a national emergency; and
> WHEREAS it is in the best interests of all bank depositors that a period of respite be provided with a view to preventing further hoarding of coin, bullion or currency, or speculation in foreign exchange
> THEREFORE I do hereby proclaim a bank holiday and that during said period all banking transactions shall be suspended...

The President made no attempt to identify the underlying causes of the crisis, merely referring to "hoarding" and "speculative activity abroad." He failed to explain hoarding as a way of protecting a life savings in the face of frequent and increasing bank insolvency coupled with no depositor insurance, or to identify speculative activity abroad as foreigners exchanging their dollar assets for gold in anticipation of dollar devaluation. Most people would understand these choices as rational, but Roosevelt labeled them "unwarranted" and "speculative" in an emotional appeal to wrongdoing. He also made no mention of government culpability or shortcomings. He could have described his proposal as a coordinated federal effort to replace the fragmented policies of different states, or a breathing period to give the government a chance to formulate new banking and monetary policies and standards. Instead, he chose to blame hoarding and speculation—individual greed. Nonetheless, the mood of the country demanded immediate action, and Roosevelt's first act as president was met with widespread approval.

EXECUTIVE AUTHORITY

Roosevelt found legal authority for his national bank holiday in legislation dating back to World War I. The Trading With the Enemy Act of October 6, 1917 gave the president the power to control all currency and banking transactions in time of war or national emergency, and to regulate or prohibit the "export, hoarding, melting, or earmarking of gold or silver coin or bullion or currency."

There are two points to be made concerning this law. First, the president does not have these powers unless specifically granted by Congress. The Constitution is clear: "The Congress shall have the power to coin Money, regulate the Value thereof, and of foreign Coin..." The power to regulate money is exclusively granted to Congress. Second, the name of the act implies an intent to delegate a wartime or national security power, not a peacetime or domestic policy authority. But Roosevelt chose to expand the meaning of "national emergency" to include a domestic banking crisis. He also chose to omit the full name of the enabling legislation, referring to it as simply "The Act of October 6, 1917" in his proclamation.

Whether or not this was a deliberately misleading omission, the nation was looking for executive leadership, and Roosevelt's legal authority went unchallenged.

FACING THE INEVITABLE

It can be argued that Roosevelt's March 6 proclamation was not so much bold as it was inevitable. Inauguration Day was Saturday, March 4. On Friday, the Federal Reserve Board advised President Hoover to declare a bank holiday on his last day in office. He was told that the banking system would be forced to close on Monday, with or without a formal declaration. But Hoover left the decision up to Roosevelt. On Saturday, with the inauguration ceremony just hours away, the New York Stock Exchange announced it was suspending operations due to a lack of bank credit for brokers. Roosevelt's only political option was to claim credit for what was going to happen anyway.

Banking professionals knew that any permanent solution would have to include both the value of the dollar and the role of gold in international banking, as well as domestic considerations such as deposit insurance and standardization of banking regulations. Roosevelt's directive avoided all of these issues, perhaps because they were too technical or too political, but most likely because he would need the cooperation and approval of Congress. He wanted his first act in office to boost public confidence by appearing authoritative and decisive, which meant leaving the more difficult decisions for later. What he needed first was for his executive authority to be firmly established.

THE EMERGENCY BANKING ACT

The use of a Presidential wartime power as executive authority for a bank holiday could have been challenged in court, so Roosevelt's first legislative request was for Congress to confirm that authority and thus avoid a possible legal battle. Part I of the Emergency Banking Act of March 9, 1933 declares:

> Section 1. The actions, regulations, rules, licenses, orders, and proclamations heretofore or hereafter taken, promulgated, made, or issued by the President of the United States or the Secretary of the Treasury since March 4, 1933, pursuant to the authority conferred by subdivision (b) of section 5 of the Act of October 6, 1917, as amended, are hereby approved and confirmed.

It then goes on to amend the act of October 6, 1917—also known as the Trading with the Enemy Act—to read "during time of war *or during any other period of national emergency declared by the President*" (emphasis added.) This gave the President the power to declare a domestic banking crisis as a national emergency.

The Emergency Banking Act was passed only three days after Roosevelt's declaration of a bank holiday. It granted authority not only for this initial action, but for any future actions the President might take under the 1917 law. Normally an exercise of power would be preceded by a granting of that power, but in this case the process was reversed, and the power was granted retroactively. The President was now authorized to pursue a more aggressive agenda.

NEW PRESIDENTIAL POWERS

The March 9 legislation, in conjunction with some amendments added two weeks later, contained a host of detailed bank regulations, including the authority of the Comptroller of the Currency to assume control over insolvent banks. These provisions were probably written by technicians from the Treasury Department or Congressional Banking Committees, not by Roosevelt's inner circle. One specific section of the act, however, was totally unexpected, and could only have been prepared at the direction of Roosevelt himself. Section 3 amends the Federal Reserve Act as follows:

> Whenever in the judgment of the Secretary of the Treasury such action is necessary to protect the currency system of the United States, the Secretary of the Treasury, in his discretion, may require any or all individuals, partnerships, associations and corporations to pay and deliver to the Treasurer of the United States any or all gold coin, gold bullion, and gold certificates owned by such individuals, partnerships, associations and corporations. Upon receipt of such gold coin, gold bullion, or gold certificates, the Secretary of the Treasury shall pay therefore an equivalent amount of any other form of coin or currency coined or issued under the laws of the United States.

Amazingly, this provision of the Emergency Banking Act gave the President, through the Secretary of the Treasury, the power to confiscate private property "in his discretion." There was no political or legal precedent, and no public discussion linking private ownership of gold to the current banking crisis, or more broadly, to three years of ongoing economic depression. Roosevelt had held office for only five days, and had never mentioned the possibility of gold confiscation during months of campaigning. Most importantly, his initial legislation incorrectly focused on gold as property, not gold as money.

REGULATING GOLD

Under a gold standard, gold is both property and money. When it takes the form of nuggets, bars, or jewelry, gold is merely property with no monetary value other than barter. When a sovereign nation mints gold coins of specific weight, fineness, and value, gold becomes both property and money. Gold derives its intrinsic value from nature, and its monetary value from government. As a coin, it has both.

The Emergency Banking Act gave the President the authority to regulate gold as property, when the current banking crisis only required regulation of gold as money. Two options available to Roosevelt for regulating gold as money were, first, a modification of the gold standard, and second, a revision of the official gold exchange rate, both of which had been frequent topics of discussion since 1931. John Maynard Keynes had called the gold standard a "barbarous relic," while European bankers argued that dollar devaluation was inevitable if the United States wanted to keeps its exports competitive. Modifying the gold standard, which many considered the foundation of American banking and commerce, and raising the official price of gold, which had been the same for 94 years, were radical and disruptive options that nonetheless needed to be addressed by the new president.

SUSPENDING CONVERTIBILITY

It only took one day for President Roosevelt to exercise his new authority. On March 10, the President issued an executive order temporarily suspending convertibility of the dollar into gold by prohibiting all domestic gold payments by banks and non-bank institutions alike, and restricting international gold movements and foreign exchange dealings beyond the official bank holiday. This was a severe attempt to control the currency, contradicting the very premise of a gold exchange standard, but seemed necessary to bolster local bank reserves and stem the outflow of gold from the Treasury. Most economists, who viewed the gold standard as a *policy option* of central government, rather than a *discipline* intended to restrain government, agreed.

The public, however, held a different view. They strongly supported the legal right of an individual to exchange paper money for gold (or silver, under a bimetallic standard.) The right to acquire and store gold coins was considered not only a method of saving, but also a personal safeguard against bank failure and monetary disruption or collapse. The disagreement was more political than economic, pitting government authority against individual freedom, but the two positions shared at least one thing in common: each accepted gold as both money and property. Restricting convertibility was a completely separate issue from the right to own gold.

REVISING THE GOLD EXCHANGE RATE

While Roosevelt had the authority under the Emergency Banking Act to suspend dollar-gold convertibility, he could not change the official price of gold without additional congressional approval. There was no getting around the constitutional provision that only Congress has the power to regulate the value of money.

The monetary discipline of a gold standard is maintained by an official price of gold, which is arbitrary. There is no scientific formula for arriving at a correct or optimal rate. The number is fixed, and determined by politicians, not variable as dictated by the marketplace or some other measurable factor. The benefits of a fixed rate are economic and legal certainty; the liability is a rigid standard which eventually becomes outdated.

Raising the gold exchange rate has the effect of devaluing the currency. Exports are increased because they are more competitive, and imports are decreased because they are less affordable. Gold flows inward to the Treasury, because the government is willing to pay more for it.

Roosevelt's proclamation on March 6 identified "severe drains on the nation's stocks of gold" as contributing to a national emergency. Raising the price of gold would result in an immediate increase in exports, and a net inflow of gold to the Treasury. In the long run, this form of currency control would have the greatest effect, but the Constitution gives the power to regulate the price of gold to Congress alone. The President could not rely on executive authority. The legal effects on gold as property and the economic effects on gold as money would have to be openly debated before the official gold exchange rate of $20.67 could be changed. For the moment, this provided a measure of comfort to traditional thinkers.

THE IMMEDIATE EFFECTS OF THE BANK HOLIDAY

President Roosevelt extended the bank holiday to a minimum of six days, after which most banks were allowed to resume business. Of the banks still open when the holiday was first declared, approximated 2,000 never opened their doors again. For those remaining, the panic was over, and the rush to withdraw deposits ended. This was primarily due to renewed public confidence in the banking system, but also the embargo on payments in gold. Withdrawals were limited to paper money, subsidiary coinage, and silver dollars if available.

On the international level, confidence in the American dollar improved for three reasons. First, the emergency suspension of gold payments was thought to be temporary. Second, Roosevelt made no mention of raising the official gold exchange rate, or dollar depreciation, in either his proclamations or legislation. Third, the United States still held quantities of gold more than sufficient to support the official price of $20.67. Accordingly, the price of gold on the international market stabilized, and speculation over devaluation of the dollar subsided. A period of relative calm followed, but for the American public it came to an abrupt end after only three weeks.

CRIMINALIZING GOLD – THE EXECUTIVE ORDER OF APRIL 5, 1933

President Roosevelt's next executive order was so shocking and unprecedented that it cannot be understood without quotation at length.

Executive Order of April 5, 1933
Forbidding the Private Hoarding of Gold Coin,
Gold Bullion, and Gold Certificates

By virtue of the authority vested in me by... the Act of March 9, 1933... I, Franklin D. Roosevelt, President of the United States of America, do declare that said national emergency still continues to exist and pursuant to said section do hereby prohibit the hoarding of gold coin, gold bullion, or gold certificates... from the recognized and customary channels of trade...

All persons are hereby required to deliver on or before May 1, 1933, to a Federal Reserve Bank or a branch or agency thereof or to any member bank of the Federal Reserve System all gold coin, gold bullion, and gold certificates now owned by them or coming into their ownership...

Whoever willfully violates any provision of this executive order or of these regulations or of any rule, regulation, or license issued thereunder may be fined not more than $10,000, or, if a natural person, may be imprisoned for not more than ten years, or both; and any officer, director, or agent of any corporation who knowingly participates in such violation may be punished by a like fine, imprisonment, or both.

...The following exceptions are made to the delivery requirements of this order:

(a)   Such amounts of gold as may be required for legitimate and customary use in industry, profession, or art within a reasonable time, including gold prior to refining and stocks of gold in reasonable amount for the usual trade requirements of owners mining and refining such gold.

(b)   Gold coin and gold certificates in an amount not exceeding in the aggregate $100 belonging to any one person, and gold coins having a recognized special value to collectors of rare and unusual coins.

(c)   Gold coin and bullion earmarked or held in trust for a recognized foreign government or foreign central bank or the bank for international settlements.

(d)   Gold coin and bullion licensed for other proper transactions (not involving hoarding) including gold coin and bullion imported for reexport or held pending action on applications for export licenses.

To begin, this was not simply a bureaucratic regulation establishing new rules of banking and financial conduct. It was a criminal law with stiff penalties aimed at the general population. While the order did not criminalize the ownership of gold, it forbid the "hoarding" of gold, and forced redemption by a specified date and at a rate determined by the Treasury.

Under the previous directive of March 9, convertibility was only restricted one-way—banks could not pay out gold in exchange for paper money or deposit withdrawals. This was regulation of gold as money, and was legally proper. The April 5 directive expanded restrictions on convertibility to include both directions—all persons were mandated by law to exchange their gold for paper money. This was regulating gold as property under the guise of hoarding, and was constitutionally questionable. It was certainly not the only way of discontinuing the use of gold coins as legal tender. An alternative would have been to demonetize outstanding gold coins and certificates, and cease their production at the current gold exchange rate. Once demonetized, gold coins would become mere property, like diamonds or fine art, and as property would no longer be subject to financial regulation.

REGULATION IN OTHER COUNTRIES

By the time Roosevelt assumed office, most of the world had experienced the same economic downturn as the United States, and all but a few countries had abandoned the gold standard. The way

Mexico managed the transition provides a stark contrast to Roosevelt's April 5 decree.

Since 1905, the Mexican peso had been tied to the American gold dollar at the rate of two-for-one. Mexico produced millions of 50-peso gold coins from 1921 to 1931, which were freely exchangeable at the Mexican-American border for US$25, minus transaction fees. When Mexico devalued the peso in 1932 by dropping the gold standard, they demonetized the circulating gold coinage but allowed the public to keep gold coins as bullion. After 1933, Mexican residents could own American gold coins, but American residents could not own most Mexican gold coins. There were no ill effects to the Mexican economy from maintaining private ownership of gold.

Great Britain and the commonwealth countries also handled the financial crisis quite differently from the United States. Great Britain dropped the gold standard and devalued the pound in September 1931. Gold coins had ceased to circulate in 1914 due to World War I, and were never again an important component of domestic commerce, but the British government never recalled gold coins, nor made gold ownership illegal. They did, however, promote the purchase of war bonds with gold coins as a voluntary, patriotic gesture.

The commonwealth countries of Canada, Australia, and South Africa, in addition to being important trading partners, were tied to British monetary policy in two significant ways. First, they were important producers of newly-mined gold, each on par with the California gold rush of 1849. (The 1896 "Alaskan" gold rush of

American history had, in fact, taken place in Canadian territory.) Second, the British Royal Mint operated branch facilities that produced gold sovereigns in all three countries.

The Canadian Branch Mint in Ottawa produced British gold sovereigns from 1908 to 1919, as well as Canadian $5 and $10 gold coins on the American standard from 1912 to 1914. Until 1931, Canadian, British, and American gold coins circulated freely in Canada based on availability. With British abandonment of the gold standard, the Canadian dollar lost value on the free market, and Canadian gold started flowing to New York. On December 1, 1931, the Canadian government agreed to never again produce sovereigns, and assumed control of the Ottawa mint from Britain. They also agreed to pay a world market price to Canadian miners for newly-mined gold, and placed export restrictions on raw and monetary gold. Never did the Canadian government recall gold coins or prohibit private ownership of gold. In fact, Canada became a favorite hiding place for American gold that had not been turned in under Roosevelt's order.

Australia produced British gold sovereigns at branch mints in Sydney until 1926, and Melbourne and Perth until 1931. All sovereign production ended when Britain devalued and dropped the gold standard, and Australia followed suit by devaluing its own currency. Similarly, South Africa ended production of sovereigns in 1932, abandoned the gold standard, and declared independence from Britain in 1934. Neither Australia nor South Africa ever confiscated privately-owned gold. Among the Western democracies, America was alone in this regard.

HOARDING VS. COLLECTING

The April 5 executive order made a clear exception for "gold coins having a recognized special value to collectors of rare and unusual coins." This refers to a property value that is distinct from monetary value. A coin collection is private property, and is valued by collector demand, not face value. Being an avid stamp collector himself, President Roosevelt was sympathetic to collector interests. He understood collecting to be a passionate pursuit, not a form of hoarding.

The President wanted his directive to differentiate collecting from hoarding. Both activities "withdraw and withhold gold coins from the recognized and customary channels of trade," but Roosevelt wanted hoarding to be proscribed as contributing to a national emergency, and collecting to be permitted as harmless. The distinction is unclear at best. Hoarding is a vice, but saving is a virtue. A person who keeps one coin of every type and date is a collector, but if he keeps ten of each for his ten grandchildren, his motives can be questioned. The same coin can be money or an heirloom, depending on the view of the owner. Roosevelt's exclusion of collector coins from his executive order demonstrated his understanding of the conflict between monetary regulation and property rights.

HOARDING VS. FOREIGN OWNERSHIP

The three basic methods available to President Roosevelt for regulating gold as money were limiting convertibility, changing the official dollar-gold exchange rate, and demonetizing outstanding gold coins. Each of these controls would have been universal, applying to American gold coins held both domestically and abroad.

Roosevelt's April 5 order specifically prohibited the hoarding of gold coins "within the continental United States." He sought to regulate gold as property, not money, and thus his order could not be extended abroad because he had no authority over property rights in foreign countries. Requiring foreigners to surrender their American gold coins would have been as absurd as it was unenforceable.

One of the reasons foreigners were hoarding American gold coins was the belief that devaluation, or raising the official gold-dollar exchange rate, was inevitable. By requiring only American residents to turn in their gold, Roosevelt was ensuring that any capital gains associated with a possible devaluation could be realized by foreigners, but not by Americans. Financial benefit would accrue to the American Treasury, rather than individual Americans. The United States held the largest stock of monetary and bullion gold in the world, and Roosevelt was nationalizing it at a price that would soon be wildly surpassed. As of April 5, there was no concrete evidence that Roosevelt had a specific plan to devalue the currency— but many in the financial markets were predicting that it would happen. In the business world, an executive acting on financial knowledge not fully disclosed to the public would be accused of insider trading.

EVENTS OF APRIL 20, 1933

Any doubts about Roosevelt's intentions were resolved just two weeks later. In a press conference on April 19, the President indicated that his administration would allow the American dollar to depreciate relative to foreign currencies. This was a legalistic way of saying he wanted the dollar price of gold to float, thus avoiding the Congressional approval required to raise the official dollar-gold exchange rate.

One day later, President Roosevelt issued an executive order extending the restriction on bank payments in gold, and revising the gold embargo to include all persons dealing in foreign exchange. On the same day, an amendment to the Agricultural Adjustment Act was introduced in Congress authorizing the President to reduce the gold content of the dollar. Known as the Thomas Amendment, this proposal—if adopted—would give the President the power to devalue the currency by raising the official price of gold.

The developments of April 20 ended all confidence in the value of the dollar, and resulted in an immediate increase in the world market price of gold. Over the next three months, gold traded in Europe as high as $30 per ounce, up from the official U.S. price of $20.67. European speculators and investors had been proven right:

the intrinsic value of their gold coins had increased by as much as 45%. It is impossible to believe that Roosevelt had known nothing of this outcome when he ordered the surrender of all gold coins just two weeks earlier.

THE THOMAS AMENDMENT

Three weeks after being introduced in Congress, the Thomas Amendment passed. This legislation was so important to American monetary policy, and by extension to the international gold standard, that it needs to be cited in detail.

The Thomas Amendment to the Agricultural Adjustment Act, May 12, 1933

Exercising power conferred by Section 8 of Article I of the Constitution: to coin money and regulate the value thereof.

...Whenever the President finds, upon investigation, that the foreign commerce of the United States is adversely affected by reason of the depreciation in the value of the currency of any other government or governments in relation to the present standard value of gold... the President is authorized in his discretion...

By proclamation to fix the weight of the gold dollar in grains nine-tenths fine... and to provide for the unlimited coinage of gold and silver at the ratio so fixed... but in no event shall the weight of the gold dollar be fixed so as to reduce its present weight by more than 50 per centum.

With this act, the Congress delegated its Constitutional authority to "fix the weight of the gold dollar," giving Roosevelt the power to raise the official price of gold and devalue the currency. However, the market price of gold had already risen substantially after the President announced his policy of letting the dollar float against foreign currencies, even without mention of the gold standard or the official gold exchange rate. Congress had delegated a formal authority that had already been exercised by the President in an informal and indirect way. By causing a rise in the market price, Roosevelt forced Congress to act after the fact, and raise the official dollar-gold exchange rate fixed by law. The Thomas Amendment was less a delegation of power, and more a statement of approval for the now unstoppable devaluation of the dollar.

Another significant clause in the Thomas Amendment authorized the President "to provide for the unlimited coinage of gold and silver at the ratio so fixed." The circulating gold coinage had been called in, but with this act Congress anticipated—or perhaps even encouraged—the possibility of a new gold coin issue of either lesser weight, increased face value, or both. In other words, Congress had not ruled out reinstating a full gold exchange standard at a higher price of gold. This had previously been accomplished under President Andrew Jackson in 1834, but without withdrawing the older and more valuable (under the new standard) coins from circulation. There is no evidence that Roosevelt entertained this possibility.

ABROGATION OF THE GOLD CLAUSE – JUNE 5, 1933

Less than four weeks after granting President Roosevelt the power to officially devalue the dollar, Congress passed a joint resolution nullifying all contractual obligations for payment in gold or gold coin. It reads in part:

Joint Resolution to Assure Uniform Value to the Coins and Currencies of the United States.

WHEREAS the holding of or dealing in gold affect the public interest, and are therefore subject to proper regulation and restriction; and

WHEREAS the existing emergency has disclosed that provisions of obligations which purport to give the obligee a right to require payment in gold or a particular kind of coin or currency of the United States, or in an amount of money of the United States measured thereby, obstruct the power of the Congress to regulate the value of money of the United States and are inconsistent with the declared policy of the Congress to maintain at all time the equal power of every dollar, coined or issued by the United States, in the markets and in the payment of debts. Now therefore be it

RESOLVED – that every provision contained in or made with respect to any obligation which purports to give the obligee the right to require payment in gold or a particular kind of coin or currency, or in an amount in money of the United States measured thereby, is declared to be against public policy; and no such provision shall be contained in or made with respect to any obligation hereafter incurred. Every obligation, heretofore or hereafter incurred, whether or not any such provision is contained therein or made

with respect thereto shall be discharged upon payment, dollar for dollar, in any coin or currency which
at the time of payment is legal tender for public and
private debts.

The resolution goes on to amend the act of May 12, 1933, to
read as follows:

All coins and currencies of the United States (including Federal Reserve notes and circulating notes of
Federal Reserve banks and national banking associa-
tions) heretofore or hereafter coined or issued, shall be
legal tender for all debts public and private, public
charges, duties, and dues, except that gold coins, when
below the standard weight and limit of tolerance provided by law for the single piece, shall be legal tender
only at valuation in proportion to their actual weight.

The abrogation of the Gold Clause had by far the largest economic effect of any of Roosevelt's gold policies or restrictions.
Most bonds issued during the previous ten years—including those
of states and municipalities, railroads, industrial concerns, and public utilities—contained the clause "in gold coin of the United States
of America of or equal to the present standard of weight and fineness." Even the United States Treasury issued bonds containing
similar wording. If all these obligations were paid off with gold
coins worth significantly more than face value (due to devaluation),
the transfer of wealth—albeit from one wealthy group to another—would have been staggering. Senator Thomas of Oklahoma,
who introduced this resolution, estimated its effect at over $200
billion. By comparison, the total worth of all monetary gold in the

United States at the time was just over $4 billion, or 2% of the potential exposure. This resolution expanded the conflicts inherent in Roosevelt's monetary and gold policies well beyond property rights; they now included rights and obligations under contract law. Gold Clause litigation began immediately, and appeared before the Supreme Court two years later. The results of these cases will be discussed in detail in Part II.

A lesser-known effect of this resolution was the revaluation of American gold coins from face value to gold value. A $20 gold coin retained its legal tender status, but no longer at the nominal $20. Its value would now be determined by the official value of the gold content, to be set at a later date as authorized by the Thomas Amendment. This ensured that gold coins would continue to be regulated as money, even if they were no longer circulated or used as money; whereas devaluation, or removal of legal tender status, would have reduced gold coins to property and limited the possibilities for government control. With each new executive order or act of Congress, it appeared that Roosevelt was using the Constitutional authority to control monetary gold as a pretense to confiscate and even criminalize all privately-owned gold held as a store of value.

CRIMINALIZING OWNERSHIP OF GOLD – THE EXECUTIVE ORDER OF AUGUST 28, 1933

Up to this point, many Americans believed President Roosevelt's gold policies were temporary, based on a literal interpretation of "national emergency." The requirement to exchange gold coins for paper money was considered to be a civic duty, much like a military draft or income surtax during time of war—measures that would be reversed at war's end. Even Congress anticipated an eventual return to a gold exchange standard, as indicated by the "unlimited coinage of gold and silver" clause in the Thomas Amendment. It was expected that Roosevelt's drastic measures to stabilize the banking system would be followed by a return to normalcy in the currency standard.

The Executive Order of April 5 prohibited the hoarding of gold coins without going so far as to criminalize actual ownership of gold. Less than five months later, however, Roosevelt amended this edict and fundamentally altered its meaning by adding a single word. The Executive Order of August 28, 1933, included the following provisions:

> Sec. 5. Holding of Gold Coin, Gold Bullion, and Gold Certificates... After 30 days from the date of this order, no person shall hold in his possession or retain any interest, legal or equitable, in any gold coin, gold bullion, or gold certificates situated in the United States and owned by any person subject to the jurisdiction of the United States, except under license therefore issued pursuant to this Executive Order...

Sec. 10. Whoever willfully violates any provision of this Executive Order of any license, order, rule, or regulation issued or prescribed hereunder, shall, upon conviction, be fined not more than $10,000 or... imprisoned for not more than 10 years, or both...

With this new order, the crime of "hoarding" was expanded to include "holding," clearly defined as mere possession as well as outright ownership. Roosevelt had declared gold coins to be contraband, putting them in the same category with heroin and hand grenades. The pretense of a national emergency was once again used to promote an anti-gold agenda, this time going well beyond simple regulation and placing grave doubt on any use of the word "temporary."

The legality of the August 28 executive order was quickly challenged in the courts, and Section 5 was initially held to exceed the authority delegated to the President by Congress. Before the appeals process could play out, however, Congress passed the Gold Reserve Act on January 30, 1934, clarifying earlier Congressional intent and codifying the practical effects of the President's order without need for the order itself to be ruled legal. Soon after, the case was dropped and never brought before the Supreme Court. In the 1960s, the issue was again raised, based on the assertion that any national emergency which may have existed in 1933 had long since passed. This later challenge will be discussed in detail in Part II.

A NEW OFFICIAL PRICE FOR GOLD

In 1834, the United States had fixed the official price of gold at
$20.67 per troy ounce.[1] The dollar was backed by gold at this rate
for the next 99 years, with one short interruption: in order to finance the Civil War, the North was forced to issue greenbacks—
the nation's first experiment with paper money—and suspend the
gold standard. From 1862 to 1879, the value of the paper dollar
floated with the fortunes of war and recovery, while the mint continued to produce gold coins at the official standard, creating a
two-tier system of currency. In 1879, fixed payment in gold was
resumed at pre-war levels, and a single system of currency emerged.
From that date until 1933, the official gold exchange rate of $20.67
was continuously maintained. The integrity of the system was upheld despite the most severe "national emergency" imaginable.

In the fall of 1933, the Roosevelt administration broke with the
tradition of a fixed dollar-gold exchange rate. After passage of the
Thomas Amendment in May, the world market price of gold had
become unstable, fluctuating as much as 50% in less than four
months, while the official price of gold set by the Treasury Department remained the same. On September 8, the Treasury announced that the official gold-dollar exchange rate would hence-

---

[1] For those interested in exact calculations, the law as passed in 1834 and supple-
mented in 1837 set the official weight of a United States $10 gold coin at 258
grains of .900 fine gold, which is equivalent to 232.2 pure grains fine gold. At 480
grains per troy ounce, this is equal to .4838 of a troy ounce for $10, or $20.67 for
one troy ounce.

forth be allowed to float, based on a daily fixing of estimated world market prices less shipping and insurance costs. The Treasury would buy gold from American miners and foreign interests at these increased levels, but American "holders" of gold coins and bullion would continue to be compensated at the old fixed rate of $20.67 per ounce.

Devaluing the dollar relative to gold created contradictions among the administration's other gold policies. Under the Emergency Banking Act, the President could require the surrender of all gold coins to the Treasury, and the Secretary of the Treasury would "pay therefore an equivalent amount of any other form of coin or currency." This meant that a $20 gold coin would be compensated with a $20 bill. However, the Thomas Amendment—as amended itself by the June 5 Joint Resolution—provided that gold coins "shall be legal tender only at valuation in proportion to their actual weight." This was done so that in the event of gold-dollar devaluation, the holders of contractual obligations payable in gold coin would only be compensated with coins of modified legal tender value, not of coins with gold value much greater than legal tender value. For the current holders of gold coins, the increase in legal tender value should have likewise applied, and the Treasury should have compensated every holder of gold coins after September 8 at an increased (floating) rate. Of course, this never happened. It was now obvious that the implied—but as yet unstated—intentions of the President were first to confiscate privately-owned gold, and then to ensure any increases in the value of gold accrued to the Treasury, rather than individuals.

OFFICIAL MARKET INTERVENTION

The Treasury's decision to let the official gold-dollar exchange rate float was a bold experiment in monetary policy. By relying on market forces rather than an arbitrary standard, the government was in effect ceding direct control over the value of its currency. It didn't take long for Treasury officials to have second thoughts. By early October, the administration was actively intervening in world gold markets in an attempt to manipulate prices. The Treasury Department worked in concert with the Reconstruction Finance Corporation and the Federal Reserve to buy foreign gold at progressively higher prices. The daily fixing used as a benchmark for purchasing newly-mined domestic gold was derived from these foreign transactions. The official gold-dollar exchange rate was being managed, not floated.

By importing gold, and exporting dollars at various controlled levels, the Treasury was collecting data and observing market reactions to a variety of gold-dollar exchange rates. The administration was effectively applying a trial and error process to devaluation as an alternative to a purely political decision or an arbitrary executive mandate. An eventual return to some form of gold standard was assumed, but the technical details, including an appropriate fixed price for gold, were still unresolved.

NATIONALIZING THE GOLD SUPPLY – DECEMBER 28, 1933

The gold policies of President Roosevelt over a ten-month period provided a classic example of a political slippery slope. On April 5, the President declared "hoarding" to be illegal, and on August 28 the crime was elevated to "holding." On December 28, 1933, the Secretary of the Treasury finalized the mandate by "requiring the delivery of gold coin, gold bullion, and gold certificates to the Treasurer of the United States" (that is, from the theoretically-temporary hands of the banks into the more permanent possession of the government itself.) This is the definition of confiscation; it merely took ten months to be so stated.

The terms of the order substantially mimicked the earlier orders of March 9, April 5, and August 28, often employing identical wording with the added phrase, "to pay and deliver to the Treasurer of the United States." The order was signed by H. Morgenthau, Jr., the acting Secretary of the Treasury, with an approval below from Franklin D. Roosevelt. It was also accompanied by a cover letter from Wm. McC. Martin, Governor of the Federal Reserve Bank of St. Louis, urging all banking institutions to contact each customer "whom you have any reason to believe holds any gold coin, gold bullion, or gold certificates" required to be delivered. Thus the nationalization of the gold supply was ordered with the full authority and approval of the President, the Treasury Secretary, and the Federal Reserve. Ratification by Congress had yet to be sought.

THE PRESIDENT REQUESTS LEGISLATION – JANUARY 15, 1934

Less than three weeks after nationalizing the publicly-held gold supply by executive action, President Roosevelt submitted a formal written request to Congress "to organize a sound and adequate currency system." Extracts from this document follow:

> I ask the Congress for certain additional legislation to improve our financial and monetary system. By making clear that we are establishing permanent metallic reserves in the possession and ownership of the federal government, we can organize a currency system which will be both sound and adequate...
>
> Certain lessons seem clear. For example, the free circulation of gold coins is unnecessary, leads to hoarding, and tends to a possible weakening of national financial structures in times of emergency. The practice of transferring gold from one individual to another or from the government to an individual within a nation is not only unnecessary, but in every way undesirable.
>
> Therefore it is a prudent step to vest in the government of a nation the title to and possession of all monetary gold within its boundaries and to keep that gold in the form of bullion rather than coin.
>
> Because the safe-keeping of this monetary basis rests with the government, we have already called in the gold which was in the possession of private individuals or corporations. There remains, however, a very large weight in gold bullion and coins which is still in the possession or control of the Federal Reserve Banks.
>
> Although under existing law there is authority, by executive act, to take title to the gold in the possession or control of the Reserve Banks, this is a step of such

importance that I prefer to ask the Congress by specific enactment to vest in the United States government
title to all supplies of American-owned monetary
gold...

Such legislation places the right, title, and ownership to our gold reserves in the government itself; it
makes clear the government's ownership of any added
dollar value of the country's stock of gold which
would result from any decrease of the gold content of
the dollar which may be made in the public interest...

With the establishment of this permanent policy,
placing all monetary gold in the ownership of the government as a bullion base for its currency, the time has
come for a more certain determination of the gold
value of the American dollar.

After four months campaigning as the Democratic Party nomi-
nee, another four months as President-elect, and ten months as
President, Roosevelt finally stated (or perhaps admitted) his policies on gold in a clear fashion: nationalize all monetary gold and
gold bullion, including Federal Reserve holdings, and ensure any
increase in the value of that gold due to dollar devaluation accrues
to the Treasury, not to individuals. A point-by-point analysis of the
President's Congressional request is appropriate.

1.) The President requested legislation "to improve our financial
and monetary system" by "establishing permanent metallic reserves
in the possession and ownership of the federal government." In
fact, the Federal Treasury had always maintained sufficient gold
reserves to accommodate shifts in foreign payments and trade imbalances. What the President actually called for was a federal government monopoly on gold ownership.

2.) The President flatly stated, "certain lessons seem clear. The free circulation of gold coins is unnecessary..." This is true. Most economies in 1933 functioned adequately without legal tender gold coins in circulation. But he went on to say, "transferring gold from one individual to another... is not only unnecessary, but in every way undesirable." This last point is absurd. Transferring privately-owned gold has little to do with the necessity of circulating legal tender gold coins. Gold in the form of nuggets, bars, foreign coins, or privately-minted medals are merely property, not legal tender, and using such property as gifts or as barter for value received can never be construed as "in every way undesirable." Roosevelt confiscated all bullion gold, not just legal tender gold.

3.) Roosevelt considered it "prudent" to keep all confiscated gold "in the form of bullion rather than coin." This meant that the coins would be melted, rather than demonetized. Gold coins still outstanding would continue to be legal tender, and subject to government control.

4.) Up to this point, Roosevelt's restrictions on the private ownership of gold made no mention of the gold held by the Federal Reserve. In fact, the President depended on the Federal Reserve to assist in the execution of his policies. Americans were ordered to turn in their gold to a member bank of the Federal Reserve System, or directly to a Federal Reserve bank or branch. Apparently, Roosevelt thought the institution was too powerful, too important, or both, to order the nationalization of all gold held in Federal Reserve vaults on executive authority alone. He therefore sought political cover by requesting Congressional approval in the form of legislation. Whether this "step of such importance" was a deferential act of respect, or a cleverly disguised power play, is a subject for debate.

5.) Lastly, the President asked Congress "for a more certain determination of the gold value of the American dollar." This followed a three-month period of floating dollar-gold exchange rates, as pursued by Roosevelt's Treasury Department. The President wanted to devalue the dollar, but did not want to be responsible for establishing the fixed rate. He did, however, want to "make clear the government's ownership of any added dollar value of the country's stock of gold which would result from any decrease of the gold content of the dollar." Finally, a clear statement of Presidential intentions, ex post facto.

THE GOLD RESERVE ACT – JANUARY 30, 1934

It took only 15 days for Congress to act on Roosevelt's request "to protect the currency system of the United States." The Gold Reserve Act was the culmination of the President's gold policies, and served to codify most of his executive orders as well as accommodate his legislative requests.

The first and most extensive portion of the act ordered the nationalization of all gold held by the Federal Reserve. The Treasury would issue gold certificates as a receipt for all gold tendered, and allow these certificates to be counted as part of the bank's reserve requirements. In essence, the government swapped physical assets for accounting credits. America's central bank was treated more or less the same as an ordinary citizen, with the important distinction that this was confiscation by legislation, not by executive authority.

The Gold Reserve Act goes on to specify many other provisions involving the American monetary system, including some governing the use of silver as a monetary metal, but the following items are most relevant to the subject of gold confiscation:

1.) The Secretary of the Treasury would be given the responsibility for determining and enforcing all gold regulations, but the act made no specific reference to the legality of "holding" gold. This aspect of Roosevelt's gold policies would remain as an executive order only.

2.) Enforcement of all regulations would be accompanied by forfeiture of any gold involved and financial penalties equal to twice the value of all gold seized.

3.) The United States would cease production of all gold coins for domestic use, but would continue to produce gold coins for foreign governments.

4.) All gold coins would be removed from circulation and melted into bar form.

5.) Any increase in the value of gold due to devaluation of the dollar would accrue to the Treasury, and be treated as a "miscellaneous receipt" for accounting purposes.

6.) Out of the "miscellaneous receipts" available to the Treasury, a "stabilization fund" in the amount of $2 billion would be created for use by the Executive Branch. This fund would be:

...under the exclusive control of the Secretary of the Treasury, with the approval of the President, whose decisions shall be final and not be subject to review by any other officer of the United States. The fund shall be available for expenditure, under the direction of the Secretary of the Treasury, and in his discretion, for any purpose in connection with carrying out the provisions of this section, including the investment and reinvestment in direct obligations of the Unites States of any portions of the fund which the Secretary of the Treasury, with the approval of the President, may from time to time determine are not currently required for stabilizing the exchange value of the dollar.

In other words, the primary purpose of the "stabilization fund" was not to stabilize the exchange value of the dollar, but rather to authorize the President to use the increase in value of the recently-nationalized gold supply to finance up to $2 billion in government expenditures not covered by tax receipts. This was one method used to finance New Deal deficit spending. (Others, including the use of the Social Security Trust Fund, are well beyond the present discussion.)

7.) Lastly, the Gold Reserve Act amended the Thomas Amendment to set the minimum dollar value of gold at $34.45 (technically, .2902 troy ounce per U.S. dollar.) The day after enactment, Roosevelt announced an official dollar-gold exchange rate of $35.00, where it would remain until the Nixon administration. With devaluation of the dollar accomplished, the Presidents gold policies were fully realized: in less than 11 months, he had fundamentally transformed the monetary system of the wealthiest nation on Earth.

SUMMARY AND CONCLUSIONS

On January 31, after officially devaluing the dollar, President Roosevelt issued a detailed explanation of the gold policies that had already been put in place, including a ten-point statement of aims and objectives. The first eight points referenced income stability, market fluctuations, cost of living, stable employment, value of the dollar, stable exchange rates, and international payment mechanisms. All of these subjects were the proper pursuits of an active Treasury Department in the management of a gold-based monetary system. However, the President concluded his list of objectives with the following two points:

> 9.) To restrict the "unjustified enrichment" – the unearned profit from gold and foreign exchange – which at other times here and at all times in most other nations was permitted to fall to a privileged few as a result of governmental monetary action.
>
> 10.) To make more effective the control of our monetary system and of the metallic reserves of gold and silver used as its base; and to make clear that it belongs where the Constitution says it does – in the Congress rather than in the hands of the bankers and the speculators.

These last two objectives were offered as if they had been obvious all along. In fact, both were stated here for the first time, and only after all of Roosevelt's policies had been enacted. To begin, the President had never acknowledged he was calling in all gold coins and gold bullion to restrict "unjustified enrichment," which by his own admission was permitted to occur in the past both domestically (since 1834 under Andrew Jackson) and abroad (at all times, just as he stated.) Even the use of such a derogatory phrase questions the very foundation of private property rights, and could be applied as well to any real estate, stock, bond, or patent transaction resulting in a profit to the seller. This kind of language would never have been acceptable to the public, as it was not just the "privileged few" who held gold as insurance against bank insolvency and monetary uncertainty.

Additionally, Roosevelt failed to mention that the same so-called "unjustified enrichment" would be placed in the hands of the Executive Branch, where it would be used to finance the President's New Deal agenda. In effect, Roosevelt had placed a 100% capital gains tax on gold, but concealed his true objective until after the fact.

Objective 10 again confuses gold as money and gold as property. Certainly the Constitution gives control of the monetary system to Congress—and in particular, control over the price of gold and silver—but nowhere does it state or imply that such control extends to the private ownership of gold. The metallic reserves of the nation are the nation's property, but are quite distinct from gold and silver owned by the public. Ownership of gold in 1933 was not limited to "bankers and speculators"—it was a part of everyday life for farmers, merchants, contractors, laborers, and anyone else who had no other reliable way of protecting their money, particularly those on the western frontier. There was, and is, no constitutional basis for the nationalization of all privately-owned gold. Roosevelt skirted the issue by referring to Constitutional "control," when in fact the primary constitutional issue was confiscation.

President Roosevelt was responsible for a remarkable set of accomplishments in his first term, including securities regulation, banking reform, and social security. Implementation of the gold agenda was only a small part of his overall achievements, but it nonetheless revealed considerable political skill. On the first day in office, he declared a bank holiday that was otherwise inevitable, like a crowing rooster taking credit for the sunrise. Five days later, he used the popularity of his holiday to push through legislation that legalized his actions after the fact. The proverb "better to beg forgiveness than ask permission" was a frequent tactic of the President: he took away the gold before devaluation, knowing the reverse would result in much lower compliance; he devalued the currency informally by allowing it to float, forcing a formal devaluation with the passage of the Thomas Amendment; he manipulated the price of gold without declaring an official rate, forcing Congress to make the final decision; and finally, he withheld all intentions of using "unjust enrichment" as justification for a New Deal financial scheme until after the passage of the Gold Reserve Act.

The success of Roosevelt's gold policies were a result of timing, gradualism, and a deft reading of the public and Congress. By modern standards his achievement was incredible—most especially because of how few words of legislation were required to do it. Compare that to recent government efforts such as the Dodd-Frank Banking Regulation, with pages numbering in the thousands.

Even with this obvious success, however, a number of basic questions remain concerning Roosevelt's gold policies in particular.

1.) **Why did he have such obvious disdain for the public use, possession, and ownership of gold?** A brief list of his choice of words leaves no doubt: "unwarranted withdrawals" for the "purpose of hoarding"... "extensive speculative activity"... the transfer of gold being "in every way undesirable"... the "unjustified enrichment" of a "privileged few"... gold assumed to be in the hands of only "bankers and speculators." These are not the words of a man merely looking for monetary stability, but of one determined to right a moral wrong.

2.) **Was his attitude toward gold deeply rooted, and thus actively concealed from the public prior to inauguration, or was it just an immediate and practical response to the banking crisis of January 1933?** If the President had touted a policy of confiscation prior to election, he would have given Hoover substantial political ammunition, perhaps leading to a populist backlash. It certainly would have cost him votes, as well as given time for opposition to his ideas to develop. While it is dangerous to question a politician's inner motives, it is also difficult to understand how such a well-executed effort against gold could have been conceived and developed in a matter of weeks. In researching this book, the author found no good evidence as to the origin of Roosevelt's ideas concerning confiscation of gold. What is undeniable is that, aside from Stalinist Russia, no other major country had adopted such a policy in the 20th century.

3.) **Was confiscation necessary?** Roosevelt's entire anti-gold campaign was based on a declaration of "national emergency," using similar language in at least five of his executive orders. The simplest explanation of this emergency was a nationwide run on the banks and an unmanageable demand for gold. In the short run, the problem was met with temporary bank closures and suspension of all payments in gold. The emergency was soon quelled, and most banks reopened under stricter controls, while the weaker banks were liquidated. The short-run measures were successful, buying time for long-run solutions. But was gold confiscation a necessary part of a long-term solution? Ironically, the single most important banking reform offered during the first year of Roosevelt's administration had nothing to do directly with gold policy. The Banking Act of 1933, which became effective January 1, 1934, created the Federal Deposit Insurance Corporation (FDIC), which offered deposit insurance to all Federal Reserve member banks as well as any non-member banks wanting to participate. The primary cause of bank runs was a lack of deposit insurance when depositors doubted the solvency of their bank, and thus the safety of their deposits. Upper limits notwithstanding, FDIC insurance solved this problem for small- and medium-sized accounts, and provided the widespread public confidence necessary for an orderly banking system.

Meanwhile, the problem of unmanageable gold withdrawals, labeled by the President as "hoarding," was caused by a loss of confidence, both domestic and international, in the gold value of the American dollar. It was solved by suspension of gold payments in the short run, and dollar devaluation in the long run.

So, how did gold confiscation contribute to a long-run solution to the "national emergency?" In short, it was unnecessary and contributed nothing. Gold coins could have been significantly withdrawn from circulation prior to devaluation by simply maintaining a one-way gold window at all banks—deposits only, no withdrawals, all voluntary. This strategy was successfully applied by the Federal Reserve from September 1917 until the end of World War I, coincident with the Trading With the Enemy Act of October 6, 1917. It has also been Federal Reserve policy in modern times for $500 and $1000 bills for many years.

Upon devaluation of the currency, the outstanding gold coins could have been demonetized or not, but left in either case with their owners, to be traded as bullion or collectibles on the open market. This was the way it was managed by many countries for decades—including the United States in 1834—providing a number of successful examples to follow. The only loss to the government with this strategy would have been a portion of the "stabilization fund" being used to finance New Deal spending, the magnitude of which would have equaled the "unjustified enrichment" realized by United States residents who opted to keep their gold coins rather than deposit them voluntarily. Roosevelt would have had to find a more transparent method of finance for his deficit spending.

The tradeoffs for gold policy were relatively clear: increased government revenue and complete government control of the nation's gold, versus property rights and economic freedoms. While these were proper issues for the government to consider, they were resolved in an authoritarian manner, with very little public notice, debate, or participation.

KENNETH R. FERGUSON

PART II:

GOLD AS CONTRABAND

II.

PUBLIC COMPLIANCE

Both the prohibition of alcohol and the confiscation of gold were laws that criminalized the ordinary behavior of otherwise law-abiding citizens. It is oddly coincidental that the end of one should have been so close to the beginning of the other. The 21st Amendment to the Constitution repealing prohibition was adopted on December 5, 1933, less than two months before the Gold Reserve Act became law. A major difference between the two events was that President Roosevelt campaigned on a platform of prohibition repeal, while making no mention of gold confiscation prior to the election.

Since the alcohol laws were reversed largely due to a lack of public compliance, it seems appropriate to consider the confiscation of gold in these same terms. Were Roosevelt's efforts to nationalize the gold supply by confiscation effective? Could the level of public compliance with the gold laws be measured? And was it ever feasible for the government to enforce a gold-as-contraband policy?

According to Federal Reserve records, the total face value of all outstanding gold coin as of February 1933 was $571 million. At the end of January 1934—after Roosevelt had called in all gold coin and devalued the dollar—the amount of gold coin still outstanding was $287 million, or slightly more than 50%. The other half, which had presumably been returned in accordance with the April 5 edict, can be classified into four categories:

1.) Gold coin held by banks as vault cash, turned in via the Federal Reserve.

2.) Gold coin held by the Federal Reserve, subsequently turned in to the Treasury in compliance with the Gold Reserve Act.

3.) Gold coin deposited by the public without coercion, as a part of normal business activity.

4.) Gold coin surrendered to banks by the public against their will, in compliance with Roosevelt's gold laws.

Our immediate concern is only with category four above. How much gold was surrendered to the government involuntarily, as opposed to the amount withheld in violation of the law? There are no exact figures, but it can be safely assumed to be less than $284 million, given that the other three categories must account for some portion of the total deposits.

By comparison, the gold coin still outstanding after the passage of the Gold Reserve Act—totaling $287 million according to the Federal Reserve—can be accounted for as follows:

1.) Gold coin lost, destroyed, or melted – Altogether this amount is insignificant. Coins would only have been melted in quantity after devaluation, not before.

2.) Net exports of gold coin prior to April 5, 1933 – This includes gold held by foreign banks and wealthy individuals for purposes of speculation. The amount is unknown, but tempered by the fact that speculators could hold gold coins from any other country to the same end.

3.) Gold coin smuggled abroad after April 5, 1933 – The most frequent destination for gold smuggled out of the United States in defiance of Roosevelt's gold laws was Canada, due to the long, open border as well as their stable political and banking system. In most cases, the gold ended up in Canadian bank safe deposit boxes, but Canada was also a staging area for shipment to other countries.

4.) Gold illegally withheld by the public – This last category includes all gold coin and gold bullion hidden from authorities inside cookie jars, under mattresses, and buried in flower gardens. On page 464 of *A Monetary History of the United States 1867-1960*, Friedman and Schwartz conclude that "the bulk of the $287 million was retained illegally in private hands."

If we add together the amount of gold smuggled with the amount retained illegally in private hands (numbers 3 and 4 above), it can be surmised that the total amount of gold withheld in violation of the law was at least as great as the amount voluntarily surrendered to the government, thus setting the level of compliance between April 1933 and January 1934 at no more than 50%. Whether this number represents a governmental success or failure is left for the reader to decide.

There are, however, two additional factors to consider when estimating compliance rates. First, the total face value of all gold coins turned in to the Treasury between 1934 and 1960 was less than $12 million, or roughly 4% of the total outstanding as of January 1934. Nearly all of this was reclaimed through discovery and seizure rather than voluntary surrender, so it's clear that the early rates of noncompliance held steady even after the passage of the Gold Reserve Act. Second, the Federal Reserve figures only account for United States legal tender gold coins. There is no way to estimate compliance regarding gold contraband generally classified as bullion, which includes bars, medallions, nuggets, and most importantly, foreign coins. The United States was a nation of immigrants, and what wealth they had was often brought over in various forms of gold and precious stones. Given this, the level of compliance was almost certainly much lower than 50%. As with other black markets, the market for owning, trading, and smuggling contraband gold was difficult—if not impossible—for the federal government to control.

LEGAL CHALLENGES

For four days beginning January 8, 1935, the Supreme Court heard arguments for a trio of cases that formed the greatest legal challenge to Roosevelt's gold laws, collectively known as the Gold Clause cases. These legal actions sought to overturn the Joint Resolution of June 5, 1933, which nullified all contractual obligations for specific payment in gold or gold coin. This resolution, commonly cited as the Abrogation of the Gold Clause, had the greatest economic impact among all of Roosevelt's gold restrictions. Each of the Gold Clause cases is briefly described below.

1.) *Norman v. Baltimore and Ohio Railroad Co.* – arguing that payment of a corporate bond containing a gold clause must be paid in gold coin or gold equivalent, not legal tender or paper money equivalent.

2.) *Nortz v. United States* – arguing that a gold certificate issued by the United States is an explicit agreement between the government and the bearer for payment in gold coin.

3.) *Perry v. United States* – arguing that a government bond containing a clause for payment of principle and interest in gold must be honored with gold.

The Supreme Court chose to hear these cases because each represented a specific category of dispute arising from a gold clause. The first concerned a private debt obligation, the second a guarantee of government-issued currency, and the third a promise of government debt repayment. The precedents for these cases were long and deep. Contract law governing private obligations for "payment in gold" dated back to the Civil War and the greenback era. Gold notes issued by the Treasury contained the specific declaration, "payable in gold coin," and were intended to be backed by the "full faith and credit" of the United States. Then, in 1900, the nation finally rejected bimetallism by pegging the value of the dollar to a fixed weight of gold, and shortly thereafter declaring that all government bonds should contain a contract to pay in gold. Even after the April 5, 1933 executive order criminalizing the hoarding of gold and demanding its surrender, the government sold $500 million in bonds with a guarantee for payment in gold on May 2 of that year.

Arguments for both sides of the Gold Clause cases were supported by scores of legal decisions, mostly involving the definitions of "payment," "money," and "legal tender." The real dispute, however, was not found in complex and arcane legal arguments, but rather in the perceived economic and political consequences of a judgment either way. The hard truth was that upholding all gold clause obligations could have resulted in national bankruptcy. The oral arguments of the Attorney General contained the following:

> To admit such claims to the extent of $100,000,000,000 [$100 billion], an unthinkable sum, would be to write up the public debts and the private debts of our country by $69,000,000,000 [$69 billion] and, overnight, reduce the balance of the Treasury of the United States by more than $2,500,000,000 [$2.5 billion]. It would add $10,000,000,000 [$10 billion] to the public debt. The increased interest charges alone would amount to over $2,500,000,000 [$2.5 billion] per annum, and that sum is twice the value of the combined wheat and cotton crops of this country in the year 1930. The stupendous catastrophe envisaged by this conservative statement is such as to stagger the imagination. It would not be a case of "back to the Constitution." It would be a case of "back to chaos."

Certainly the Constitution was not intended to be a suicide pact, but arguments for the other side were just as apocalyptic. Justice McReynolds, in a written dissent, stated:

> It is impossible to fully estimate the result of what has been done. The Constitution as many of us have understood it, the instrument that has meant so much to us, is gone. The guarantees heretofore supposed to

protect against arbitrary action have been swept away. The powers of Congress have been so enlarged that now no man can tell their limitations. Guarantees heretofore supposed to prevent arbitrary action are in the discard... Shame and humiliation are upon us now. Moral and financial chaos may confidently be expected.

Perhaps Justice McReynolds can be excused for hyperbole, but there is no doubt he stood for principle over expedience. In the end, however, principle came up short. The apparent duty of the Supreme Court was to find legal justification for disregarding principle, and save the nation from financial ruin as an unintended consequence of currency devaluation.

It is important to note, however, that the Gold Clause cases made no ruling on the legality of Roosevelt's original orders for confiscation. As Justice McReynolds noted, "The authority exercised by the President and the Treasury in demanding all coin, bullion, and certificates is not now challenged; neither is the right of the former to prescribe weight for the standard dollar. These things we have not considered." The Court upheld the legality of gold clause abrogation, but it is quite uncertain whether they would have upheld the legality of confiscation.

JOINT RESOLUTION WITHDRAWING CONSENT TO SUE

With the Gold Clause cases settled by the Supreme Court six months earlier, Congress passed a joint resolution on August 27, 1935 withdrawing consent to sue the government for claims arising from Roosevelt's gold laws. This included any suit that was:

1.) upon any gold clause securities of the United States, or for interest thereon,

2.) upon any coin or currency of the United States, or

3.) upon any claim or demand arising out of any surrender, requisition, seizure, or acquisition of any such coin or currency, or of any gold or silver.

While numbers 1 and 2 above were clearly supported by the Gold Clause court decision, number 3 was explicitly excluded from consideration, as described by Justice McReynolds. The constitutionality of gold confiscation was not then, and has never since been, adjudicated by the Supreme Court of the United States. The effect of the joint resolution was to end any claims for financial loss resulting from the gold laws, but it left open the possibility of challenging the criminal prohibitions to "holding" gold coins or gold bullion. Once again, the difference was gold as money versus gold as property. Financial losses from confiscation were one-time, and had already been realized. Crimes of possession were a continuing possibility, and could be prosecuted at any time in the future. Legal cases involving possession were, in fact, pursued into the 1960s, and will be covered later in this section.

BURGEONING GOLD RESERVES

President Roosevelt's March 6, 1933 declaration of a national emergency was in part based on "severe drains on the nation's stocks of gold." In his January 15, 1934 request to Congress concerning the proposed Gold Reserve Act and the policy of gold confiscation, the President stated, "By making clear that we are establishing permanent metallic reserves in the possession and ownership of the Federal Government, we can organize a currency system which will be both sound and adequate." History has shown that these objectives were achieved, but not by confiscating gold from the public, the banks, and the Federal Reserve. The primary reason our "permanent metallic reserves" increased from 1934 to 1940 was devaluation of the dollar, coupled with a Treasury Department policy offering to purchase any gold presented, both domestic and foreign, at the increased price of $35 per troy ounce.

Basic economics tells us that if you want to increase the supply of a commodity, you raise the price offered. This is the logic behind price supports and subsidies for farm products, natural resources, and manufactured goods such as solar panels and wind turbines. It should have been no surprise that with a 69% increase in the Treasury price for gold, world gold production increased from 25 million ounces in 1933 to 41 million ounces in 1940, and during the same period the gold stock in the Treasury increased from 200 million ounces to 630 million ounces. The United States accumulated so much of the world's gold during these few years that a special depository had to be built in 1936 adjacent to the

Fort Knox military installation in Kentucky. At the beginning of World War II, it was widely estimated that the United States owned approximately two-thirds of all central bank gold in the world. Fort Knox became an international symbol of American economic power and wealth – in the President's own words, "sound and adequate." Roosevelt's assertion that gold confiscation was necessary proved to be wrong.

A REVISED GOLD STANDARD

After the 1934 Gold Reserve Act, the United States was still on some form of gold standard, but not the gold exchange standard of 1932 and before. No one but the government could legally own gold without a license, and Treasury policy was to purchase all gold offered, both newly-mined and foreign, but to sell only to central banks in settlement of trade imbalances. The gold flows were one-way, except for government-to-government transactions. Given the quantity now in their possession, the United States could support a world gold price of $35 indefinitely.

By 1934, only seven European countries continued to support fixed exchange rates tied to gold—France, Belgium, Luxembourg, the Netherlands, Italy, Poland, and Switzerland. These countries were known as the Gold-Bloc: the last holdouts resisting competitive devaluation and abandonment of a gold standard. By the end of 1936, all seven had succumbed to the pressures of the market, and let their currencies float in an effort to reverse growing trade imbalances. The American dollar was still backed by gold at the fixed rate of $35, but it was becoming unclear whether the dollar was supported by gold, or the price of gold was supported by the dollar. Central banks were relying more and more on foreign exchange reserves as a replacement for gold reserves, and the role of gold was slowly evolving from the ultimate form of money to a mere commodity like wheat or corn.

The new monetary system created by Roosevelt and the Gold Reserve Act was called a "managed standard" by the president, with gold reserves providing the "sound and adequate" backing expected by other countries. Economist Milton Friedman characterized it somewhat differently: "Perhaps a 'discretionary fiduciary standard' is the best simple term to characterize the monetary standard which has evolved. If it is vague and ambiguous, so is the standard it denotes" (474).

In fact, the monetary system of the world was evolving from an internationally-accepted gold standard to an American dollar standard, supported by the world's largest stock of gold. Final international approval would soon be reached in 1944, at the little-known resort town of Bretton Woods, New Hampshire.

BRETTON WOODS

During President Roosevelt's tenure, there were two attempts at international cooperation and agreement concerning exchange rates, trade imbalances, debt, and economic recovery. The first was the World Economic Conference in London, convened in June 1933 in an attempt to solve the problems arising from the Great Depression. The discussions were held just two months after Roosevelt's executive order criminalizing the hoarding of privately-owned gold. Among the contributions advanced by the American delegation was a proposal to "adopt the universal rule that the authorities alone should be entitled to own gold" (Einzig 66). Apparently Roosevelt was using the conference to lobby for his gold policies beyond American borders, but objections from France and Great Britain quickly tabled the idea. According to Eichengreen, "the conference was a complete and utter failure" (317).

The second attempt at a new international monetary regime began in 1942, in anticipation of an Allied military victory that would require a worldwide rebuilding of financial structures and institutions. Perhaps the Allies learned from the failure of the World Economic Conference nine years earlier, because this effort aimed to expose difference of opinion and work toward compromises long before an actual conference took place. Representatives from Great Britain, led by John Maynard Keynes, worked together and in parallel with an American team directed by Harry Dexter White. Keynes and White held very different economic views, and it took almost two years of proposals, published plans, and negotiations before they could arrive at a formal joint statement, which would serve as a working paper for the upcoming Bretton Woods conference.

On July 1, 1944, representatives from 44 Allied nations convened in New Hampshire to work out what professor Kenneth W.

Dam called "the rules of the game." The final product, titled "Articles of Agreement of the International Monetary Fund," can be summarized in three basic categories.

1.) Creation of a Par Value System – The par value of the dollar was declared as a fixed weight of gold equal to $35 per troy ounce. The par value of all other currencies was declared in terms of dollars, to be maintained within 1% unless approved by the fund. U.S. dollars were convertible to gold, with all other member currencies convertible to any other. Deviation from currency exchange rules could result in limited access to fund resources, or expulsion.

2.) Creation of an International Monetary Fund (IMF) – All contributions to the monetary fund from member countries would be based on the size of their economy. Contributions would consist of gold in the amount of 25% of a member's quota, or 10% of its net official holdings of gold and U.S. dollars, with the balance in member currencies. The initial fund total was set at $8.8 billion. As of June 1947, $1.3 billion of that was in gold.

3.) Establishment of Fund Powers – Voting rights would be tied to the size of each member's contribution. Members could approve or disapprove of a change in parity, regulate access to fund resources, or expel other members. Loans from the fund would be made available to members for the purpose of financing current account imbalances.

The United States played a dominant role in the management of the IMF, partly due to the size of its contribution and attendant voting rights, but also from the influence of the gold-backed dollar as the preferred reserve currency. From the beginning, the British view as argued by Keynes called for a flexible role for gold, consistent with his earlier "barbarous relic" comment, while the Americans pushed for a more rigid dollar-gold standard, in large part reflecting their massive gold reserves. In an address to the House of Lords, Keynes took the contentious position that the IMF agreement was not "a gold standard," but merely "used gold as a standard of value" (Dam 96). Others commented that this was a distinction without a difference.

A practical observer might describe the IMF agreement as an indirect gold standard, with currencies convertible to dollars which could then be converted to gold. Another view would call it simply an American dollar standard. In either case, the system was based on the assumption that the United States would always honor its commitment to a gold value of $35 per ounce. This was the glue holding the agreement together.

The private ownership of gold within member countries was not addressed by the agreement. With the notable exception of Switzerland, the turmoil of war had driven European gold markets underground and made any legal restrictions foolish. Civilian populations resorted to hoarding, concealing, and smuggling gold in all forms, and at war's end, the most acceptable forms of payment on the continent were American dollars, gold coins, and barter. Much of the world was eager for a circulating gold currency, but the United States was isolated from such problems, and Roosevelt's gold policies went unchallenged.

GOLD COINS IN POSTWAR EUROPE

The demand for hard currency and gold coins in postwar Europe was intense. With the exception of Swiss francs, continental currencies were either heavily discounted, or worthless. Significant premiums were placed on easily-recognized gold coins, and barter for precious items was common. Mink coats were valued for their warmth, and silver flatware was traded for the food it was intended to service. Barbarous conflict revealed the utility of Keynes' barbarous relic.

Under the Bretton Woods agreement, the bullion value of a gold British sovereign was a little over $8, yet from 1946 to 1952, and again later, the value of a sovereign in world markets fluctuated between $10 and $13. Significant premiums over gold were also offered for Swiss 20 francs, French 20 francs, and all common American gold coins. For the moment, the value of gold coins as a preferred currency eclipsed their value as a commodity.

The postwar gold coin shortage presented a business opportunity for international minting operations, both legal and illegal. From 1949 to 1952, gold sovereigns were produced by the British Royal Mint, all dated 1925, even though the sovereign had long since been demonetized. According to Schlumberger, they were made "for use overseas" (236). Switzerland resumed production of so-called "mountain girl" 20 franc coins from 1945 to 1949, with many dated 1935, and France began re-striking 20 franc "roosters" in 1951, all dated 1907 to 1914. These were official government issues coinciding with American economic aid to Europe under the

Marshall Plan—but regardless of whether they were minted as a political and financial tool, or merely as a profitable export, two things were undeniable: first, at least three governments benefited from a hefty markup on $35 gold; second, Roosevelt's contention that the free circulation of gold coins "is in every way undesirable" was proven false.

The opportunity for profit was also noticed by counterfeiters. Illicit minting operations sprang up in Italy, North Africa, and the Middle East, while a major distribution center developed in Beirut, Lebanon. Most counterfeiters considered their enterprise "unofficial" rather than illegal, because the coins they were producing contained the proper weight of gold. They were only benefiting from the premium, not cheating on the content. One counterfeiter in Italy actually bragged that his sovereigns were better than the real ones, because they contained slightly more gold (Bloom 65).

European markets were flooded with the newly-minted counterfeits. Some were crudely made and easily recognized, while others were machine struck and of such high quality that only experts could spot them. In 1954, the West German government authorized commercial banks to begin trading in gold coins, and the problem of counterfeits was widely exposed. Alfred Dieffenbacher began collecting data on known fakes, and over many years he identified specific characteristics of hundreds of different examples of French, German, British, Swiss, and American counterfeits offered to banks throughout Europe. In 1963, he published a looseleaf collection of his research that documented the extent of the problem, and it became a critical reference tool for banks and gold dealers worldwide.

Until 1954, the counterfeits circulating in Europe and elsewhere did not appear in the United States in any quantity, because as bullion gold they were illegal to own. European bankers needed to know real from fake, but United States customs officials didn't care. Real or fake, gold coins were contraband, and could only be owned as part of a collection having "special value to collectors of rare or unusual coins." It is ironic that Roosevelt's gold laws would benefit both collectors as well as those holding gold coins illegally, by shielding them from the counterfeits plaguing Europe.

1954 GOLD REGULATION CHANGES

Under Roosevelt's April 5, 1933 executive order forbidding the private hoarding of gold, a specific exemption was made for "gold coin of recognized special value to collectors of rare and unusual coin." This provision was later carried forward by the Treasury Department as Gold Regulations section 54.20. On July 13, 1954, Treasury Secretary George M. Humphrey issued an order amending the regulations to read as follows:

Section 54.20 Rare Coin
(a) Gold coin of recognized special value to collectors of rare and unusual coin may be acquired and held, transported within the United States, or imported without the necessity of holding a license therefore.

Such coin may be exported, however, only in accordance with the provisions of Section 54.25.

(b) Gold coin made prior to April 5, 1933 is considered to be of recognized special value to collectors of rare and unusual coin.

(c) Gold coin made subsequent to April 5, 1933 is presumed not to be of recognized special value to collectors of rare and unusual coin.

The Secretary's reasoning for the changes was spelled out in his order:

> Whereas the Order of the Secretary of the Treasury of December 28, 1933, required the delivery to the United States of gold coin, except gold coin having a recognized special value to collectors of rare and unusual coin and certain other exceptions not here pertinent;
>
> Whereas twenty years have elapsed since the date of this order, a substantial portion of the gold coins known to have been in circulation on that date have been delivered in accordance with its provisions, and part of the gold coins outstanding in 1933 are known to have been held abroad and therefore not subject to the requirements of delivery;
>
> Whereas it can reasonably be assumed that substantially all of the gold coins required to be delivered under the provisions of the order have been delivered and it is not in the public interest to continue provisions requiring the individual examination of gold coins minted prior to 1933;
>
> I hereby amend the order of the Secretary of the Treasury of December 28, 1933...

Although there were good arguments for legalizing ownership of American gold coins, Secretary Humphrey's reasoning was faulty, and perhaps even contrived. His assumption that "substantially all" gold coins had been delivered failed to account for gold that was hidden domestically, or smuggled abroad in defiance of Roosevelt's orders. The implication of his order was that all remaining United States gold coins should be considered "rare and unusual," due to successful confiscation and subsequent melting. But in 1954, a United States $20 "double eagle" was among the most common monetary gold coins in the world, and still is today. They have never been rare or unusual, and as a type, they never will be.

The Secretary strained to justify his order because he was unwilling to state the obvious: the old regulations he was supposed to enforce were arbitrary, unnecessary, largely unenforceable, and contrary to international norms. He had to talk around the issue because of the profound effect the new regulations would have on private gold ownership and gold coin markets.

The Department of Labor has calculated that between 1944 and 1954, the dollar lost one-third of its purchasing power, while the price of gold set at Bretton Woods remained constant. Combined with postwar economic growth and prosperity, these conditions ensured that the Secretary's 1954 order would spark a strong revival of the gold market. The legal effects of the revised regulations included the following:

1.) All United States gold coins were now legal to own, including those hidden from authorities for 20 years, and those smuggled abroad. The ruling was, in essence, a nationwide pardon.

2.) Virtually all foreign gold coins intended for circulation, without necessarily being "rare and unusual," were now legal to own. Only seven European countries had remained on the gold standard after 1933, and by 1936 all seven had capitulated. A few countries, including the Vatican and some outside Europe, produced gold coins after 1933 for commemorative or bullion purposes, but not for circulation. In general, all gold coins actually used as money anywhere in the world were produced before April 5, 1933, and would once again be legally available to United States residents.

3.) The legal status of re-strike coins made after 1933 but dated earlier—including 1925 British sovereigns, 1907-1914 French 20 francs, and numerous coins from Austria and Hungary—was questionable, due to difficulty in recognizing re-strikes from the originals, especially by untrained government officials. As of January 1961, official gold regulations published by the Treasury Department offered no clarification, thus making the date on the coin the only determining factor in the absence of other evidence.

4.) One unintended consequence of the new regulations was that the counterfeit coins circulating in Europe and elsewhere could now make their way into American markets. Bullion traders previously barred from doing business in the United States could convert their bullion into counterfeit United States gold coins by trading with established counterfeiters. As with re-strikes, customs officials could not be expected to recognize genuine from counterfeit, especially when mixed together. The result was a flood of fake American gold coins entering the United States for over 30 years, eventually leading to the founding of the American Numismatic Association Certification Service (ANACS) as well as numerous

other private authentication services. Some of the 1950s era counterfeits are still around, and continue to plague local coin shops.

5.) While the new rules provided welcome relief from many of
Roosevelt's gold restrictions, they also created a number of cumbersome situations and contradictory interpretations. For example,
a Mexican 50 peso gold coin dated 1921-1931 was now legal, but
the same coin dated 1944-1947 was deemed contraband. Mexican
2, 2 ½, 5, 10, and 20 peso coins presented similar problems for
customs officials, with each coin requiring individual inspection. In
addition, many coins made after April 5, 1933 were truly "rare and
unusual," but the date of manufacture could be used as evidence of
contraband. Low mintage proof sets were produced from 1968 to
1974 by Colombia, Costa Rica, Haiti, and many other countries
purely as collector's items, but were subject to seizure at the border
by any customs official who only considered the dates on the coins.
Without special ruling or further inspection, only mass-produced
bullion coins of modern date and design were unquestionably prohibited, such as the South African krugerrand, or the Peru 100
soles. Clearly, counterfeit coins were also illegal, but even with
close inspection, most fakes required expert knowledge to recognize with any accuracy. Proper enforcement of the new rules was
not as simple as the Secretary's brief Rare Coin Amendment
seemed to suggest.

THE GOLD COIN LOOPHOLE

The regulation changes of 1954 were not only welcomed by traditional coin collectors, but also by gold investors who could now legally own gold for the first time in 20 years. For practical purposes, the distinction between bullion gold and collector coins under the new ruling was meaningless. As a bullion investment, gold bars were too large for the average individual, gold jewelry by weight was only popular in non-Western countries such as India and Iran, and gold nuggets were only available in remote, naturally gold-bearing regions. The preferred method of holding gold in Europe and American for hundreds of years had been legal tender coins. While they were no longer used as money, pre-1933 gold coins were still easily recognized and accepted for their honest gold value. To a government or central bank, bullion was a 400-ounce gold bar; to an individual, it was an American double eagle, a British sovereign, or a French Napoleon.

From 1933 to 1954, trade in small quantities of gold coins was not strictly policed. Local coin shops and coin conventions were allowed to operate, so long as large quantities of gold coins obviously intended as bullion did not change hands. Restrictions on imports, however, were rigidly enforced. This distinction between owning and smuggling gold was undoubtedly due to the logistics of enforcement. Restrictions on ownership at the individual level were only enforceable by local officials, who had better things to do than assess the "collector value" of a single gold coin, whereas federal customs officials were already stationed at all ports of entry and could easily enforce the gold laws. For 20 years, the gold coin trade was neither an open legal market, nor an underground black market, but something in between.

With enactment of the new regulations, the free importation of pre-1933 gold coins created a supply-side economy. Gold coins flooded into the American market, stimulating a new breed of individual investors as well as collectors. The idea of gold as a method of saving and a hedge against inflation was revived.

THE SPECTER OF INFLATION

By 1958, fears of a potential dollar devaluation were raised for the first time since the early 1930s. The British pound had already been devalued 30% in 1949, and the French franc had fallen almost 90% to a low of 500 to the dollar. The most important world reserve currency was still the gold-backed American dollar, but its value was beginning to be questioned, due to a rising balance of payments deficit, coupled with a falling national gold stock. America's gold reserves reached a peak of $24.4 billion in 1948, but by the end of 1958 were reduced to $20.6 billion, and just two years later had fallen to $17.8 billion, for a cumulative loss of 27% over 12 years.

The international pressure on America's gold reserves was increased with the rise to power of Charles de Gaulle in 1959. His desire was to restore France to international prominence by creating a sound monetary system based on a revaluation of the franc

(100 old francs = 1 new franc) as well as a massive buildup of gold reserves. Accordingly, he demanded gold for every dollar that ended up in French banks. America's balance of payments deficit was not caused by an unfavorable balance of trade, but by foreign aid, foreign investment, and the costs of military occupation forces in Europe and Asia. The intention was for these dollars to be held abroad as bank reserves, or repatriated in exchange for farm products or manufactured goods, which were plentiful and growing. Instead, the French and others were demanding gold from a rapidly depleting stock. Unless checked, a continued loss of gold reserves would result in dollar devaluation and domestic inflation. This possibility made gold look attractive as a monetary hedge.

EISENHOWER'S EXECUTIVE ORDERS

By the end of Eisenhower's term as President, the nation's gold reserves were shrinking at a rate not seen since the Banking Crisis of 1933. John F. Kennedy had already won the 1960 election, and Eisenhower only had a few weeks left to address the gold drain. On November 29, 1960, the President issued Executive Order No. 10896, citing the continued existence of a national emergency, and confirming Roosevelt's August 28, 1933 order (retroactively numbered 6260) criminalizing the holding of gold bullion within the United States. Just six weeks later, on January 14, 1961, Eisenhower issued order No. 10905 confirming Roosevelt's policy once again—but this time adding an amendment, which reads in part:

No person subject to the jurisdiction of the United States shall acquire, hold in his possession, earmark, or retain any interest, legal or equitable, in any gold coin (other than gold coin having a recognized special value to collectors of rare and unusual coin), gold certificates, or gold bullion situated outside of the United States, or any securities issues by any person holding, as a substantial part of his assets, gold as a store of value.

Since Eisenhower's two executive orders considerably overlap, they should be discussed together. First, Roosevelt's gold policies never prevented any person from holding gold *outside* the United States. Enforcement of any contraband law would require seizure, and such action on foreign soil would be problematic, if not impossible. In cases involving gold-backed securities, a paper trail might lead to prosecution within the United States, but a guilty verdict within our borders still wouldn't translate into the seizure of gold assets outside them. Eisenhower may have been hoping for voluntary compliance, but it's questionable that he ever believed his orders could be effectively enforced.

Second, both of Eisenhower's orders reference President Truman's order No. 2914 of December 16, 1950, declaring a national emergency based on the Korean War. Eisenhower was making a direct connection between a wartime national emergency rooted in the spread of international communism, and a financial national emergency based on a dwindling gold stock. The legal relevance of the Korean War to European demand for gold was tenuous, at best.

Third, even if the Korean War had once been relevant to the gold supply, the armistice had been signed a full eight years earlier in 1953. Eisenhower's orders stated the continued existence of Truman's 1950 wartime national emergency *and* Roosevelt's 1933 financial national emergency, both of which were long past by any reasonable argument. Eisenhower was making the same mistake as Roosevelt: seeking solutions to legitimate financial problems by attacking the property rights of individuals, rather than addressing the fiscal and monetary policies of the government that had caused them in the first place—and justifying his actions with dubious legal precedents.

Eisenhower's overall record on private gold ownership was mixed, and somewhat contradictory. The gold regulation changes in 1954 significantly reduced the scope of Roosevelt's prohibitions, while the January 1961 executive order expanded them. Neither change, however, had any substantial effect on the gold drain during Eisenhower's last two years in office or in subsequent years of the Kennedy administration. Under the Bretton Woods agreement, only foreign governments or their central banks could demand gold from the United States Treasury. Private ownership of gold coins or gold bullion, held domestically or abroad, had no effect on America's shrinking Treasury reserves. If blame were to be placed, it would have to be with American fiscal and monetary policy, which encouraged foreign governments to demand gold for their dollars.

TREASURY REORGANIZATION

On October 9, 1961, the Kennedy administration created a new division within the Treasury Department known as the Office of Domestic Gold and Silver Operations (ODGSO). The director of ODGSO was charged with the administration of all Treasury regulations pertaining to private ownership and transfer of gold, functions that were previously performed within the Bureau of the Mint. By transferring these functions to a separate department, the administration was signaling a renewed emphasis on regulating gold ownership.

The Director of ODGSO reported directly to the Under Secretary for Monetary Affairs, and was obligated to uphold Eisenhower's amendments to the gold regulations, including the legalization of all pre-1934 gold coins. In spite of this, President Kennedy issued executive order No. 11307, effective July 20, 1962, requiring ODGSO to issue permits for the importation of pre-1934 gold coins, in obvious contradiction to the 1954 amendments. These coins were legal to own and could easily be acquired within the United States, yet coin dealers reported that permits for importation were difficult to obtain and frequently rejected.

A possible reason for this bureaucratic bottleneck on gold imports was the fear that speculation in gold would indirectly increase the drain on national gold reserves—that is, gold imports would be financed by dollar exports, mostly to European countries, which in turn would demand Treasury gold for their dollars and deplete national reserves. Once again, the government viewed the desire to own gold as the problem, not a symptom of national policies leading to a depreciating currency.

The inequity and confusion of conflicting gold regulations would remain until the election of a new president and the replacement of cabinet officers. In a speech to the Professional Numismatists Guild, the newly-appointed Director of ODGSO, Thomas Wolfe, admitted that the permit requirement ordered by President Kennedy was ill-conceived and made no sense. On April 22, 1969, the policy was reversed.

In addition to dropping the permit requirements for importation of pre-1934 gold coins, Director Wolfe identified 148 specific foreign gold coins from 21 countries dated 1934-1959 that henceforth would be eligible for importation by permit. Most of these coins were limited-issue, non-circulating collector's items, but as a group they represented a significant expansion of legalized gold ownership under the direction of ODGSO. The administrative state was slowly unwinding Roosevelt's gold policies, without legislative participation.

CRIMINAL PROSECUTIONS

At the same time that the Treasury Department was expanding the list of permissible "gold coins of recognized special value," the Department of Justice was continuing to pursue criminal prosecution for mere possession of small amounts of gold bullion. This included cases involving gold coins not exempted as collector's items, such as Mexican 50 peso restrikes dated 1947, Chilean 100 pesos, and Peruvian 100 soles. One of these cases, heard in the District Court for Southern California in 1962, attracted a level of notoriety that was unwanted by government, but welcomed by gold advocates.

The defendants in *United States v. James Briddle and Harold Mitchell* were accused of holding approximately $700 worth of gold bullion, in violation of President Roosevelt's Executive Order 6260 of August 28, 1933. After reviewing the historical and legal basis for Roosevelt's order, district judge William C. Mathes considered the nature of the national emergency as it existed in 1933, and whether it continued to exist nearly 30 years later. As he wrote in his Memorandum of Decision dated December 27, 1962:

> Certainly a "national emergency" of an economic nature existed in 1933 at the time Executive Order No. 6260 was promulgated. The withdrawal and hoarding of gold threatened the nation's entire economy. It was against this panic that the order was directed. For this reason, the Congress obviously felt that stiff criminal penalties... were justified by the economic crisis confronting the nation.
>
> ...It is a simple matter, of course, to date the commencement of a "national emergency" by its declaration. But unless the ending be marked by proclamation also, it is sometimes difficult indeed to determine. Yet always at some point the "national emergency" does end, and the orders which find their authority in the existence of the emergency lose their validity.

Judge Mathes went on to note that this same line of reasoning was applied in a 1954 case (*Bauer v. United States*), but that the Court of Appeals refused to hear the case due to concerns over jurisdiction. Judge Mathes declared that his court was a proper jurisdiction, and that indeed a national emergency no longer existed. The defendants' motion to dismiss the indictment was granted, and the gold involved was returned to its owners.

Despite this judicial ruling, however, the government continued to prosecute cases involving the holding of gold bullion. It became obvious that in the eyes of the Justice Department, only a Supreme Court ruling or a legislative act would reverse Roosevelt's order. Judge Mathes died in 1965, and the legal precedent of his gold decision apparently died with him.

THE BRITISH EXPERIENCE

In 1947, the British government passed the Exchange Control Act, placing stringent restrictions on the ownership of gold in any form by British citizens. The act was subsequently amended to protect coin collectors by exempting all gold coins minted before 1816, as well as those minted at later dates with a numismatic value greater than their gold content value. For a brief period the regulations worked well—partly due to public cooperation and a desire for postwar economic recovery—but by 1950, it became obvious that all gold coins were selling for a considerable premium over their gold value precisely because of the government's actions. Professional coin dealers provided testimony in court that these premiums represented "numismatic value" as defined by the 1947 order, and soon the Home Office sent notice to law enforcement officials that it was no longer necessary to enforce restrictions on gold coin ownership. It was still illegal to own gold bars and other gold bullion without permit, but this had little effect on the general citizenry. The freedom to own gold was effectively restored.

From 1951 to 1966, the gold coin trade in Britain was open and generally unrestricted. By the 1960s, cost-of-living increases and general inflation similar to that experienced by the United States stimulated a renewed interest in hard assets, particularly gold. By 1966, the British government was concerned with a negative balance of payments and a drain on national monetary reserves, both gold and foreign exchange. Their solution was to reintroduce restrictions on gold coin ownership. On April 19, 1966, the British government passed a new gold coin law (Statutory Instrument 1966 No. 438), followed one week later by official "bureaucratic interpretation," a summary of recent law traditionally written in past tense:

> 1. The Treasury Department announced a general prohibition on ownership of more than four British gold coins minted after 1837. A holder of more than four gold coins could apply for exemption as a collector[2]; otherwise, any prohibited coin had to be offered

---

[2] Applicants for exemption had to not only give complete information on their gold coins minted after 1837, but also make separate filings for all other gold coins, silver coins before 1816, silver coins 1816-1919, silver coins 1920 and later, base metal coins pre-1860, and base metal coins 1860 and later. This was a paper-

for sale at the current London market price to any dealer in gold or any coin dealer specifically authorized by the Bank of England.

2. The Board of Trade declared general prohibitions to the importation of all gold coins and gold medallions less than 100 years old.

The official government justification for these measures was that they would curtail a loss of monetary reserves due to the hoarding and importation of gold, even if this loss was caused by government failure to stabilize the cost of living or slow down the rate of inflation. (Note the use of the word "hoarding" as an interchangeable pejorative for holding or owning.) Regarding the restrictions on ownership, Member of Parliament Terence L. Higgins testified before the House of Commons on June 13, 1966, "This measure is concerned purely with international transactions and, in particular, with the hoarding of gold. These clearly have no direct impact on our balance of payments... It is not only unnecessary, but it will, we suggest, prove to be unenforceable." Nonetheless, a motion to annul the statute failed 94 to 169.

Although these restrictions on gold coin ownership remained on the books for almost five years, they were, as Higgins predicted, largely unenforced. The Chancellor of the Exchequer reported to the House of Commons that after seven months there had been no prosecutions under S.I. 1966 No. 438. Another seven months later, the total had increased to two. Anecdotal evidence from London

---

work nightmare, as well as a thinly-veiled justification for owner registration and possible self-incrimination.

coin dealers indicated that enforcement was indeed soft, and that collectors were given a lot more leeway than specified by the statute. Only holders of large quantities of modern and common date sovereigns were affected. On March 31, 1971, all restrictions on ownership of gold coins were once again lifted, and import restrictions on gold coins were relaxed as well.

It can be argued that Britain's two short-lived experiments with gold coin restrictions were brought about by national emergencies similar to those faced by Roosevelt in 1933—namely, postwar reconstruction from 1947-1950, and shrinking national monetary reserves from 1966-1971. Nonetheless, there were a number of differences between the British and the American reactions to these emergencies. First, the British response was brought about by legislative action, as opposed to executive mandate. Second, the British lawmakers were open to public debate and review, as well as subsequent correction in a democratic and timely manner. Third, the restrictions on gold ownership were relatively limited in duration, implying that the emergency eventually ceased to exist. In fact, Britain became the first major partner in the Bretton Woods agreement to devalue its currency in November 1967, thus admitting that gold as property was not the problem, but rather the government's economic and monetary policy. These differences provide a stark contrast to Roosevelt's gold laws before devaluation, and their management after the Gold Reserve Act and official devaluation in 1934.

EROSION OF THE GOLD DISCIPLINE

The Bretton Woods agreement was a compromise between the discipline of a gold exchange standard and the flexibility of a managed fiduciary standard. The result was a hybrid arrangement that could accurately be called a gold-backed American dollar standard. The integrity of the entire system was based on the reliability of the gold-dollar relationship. As long as the dollar was sufficiently backed by gold, the rest of the world could substitute dollars for gold for purposes of currency valuation and central bank reserves. Never in history had the paper money of one country been given such value and respect.

Unfortunately, the integrity of the gold-dollar relationship began to erode less than one year after the adoption of Bretton Woods, and even before the end of World War II in the Pacific. On June 12, 1945, the House and Senate amended the Federal Reserve Act to reduce the required gold reserves against notes outstanding from 40% to 25%, and the required gold reserves against deposits from 35% to 25%. Undoubtedly, one purpose of this legislation was to increase the availability of dollars for the reconstruction of war-torn Europe. The good intentions of rebuilding a peaceful Europe outweighed any fear of inflation or social disruption to come. Inflation was seen as an acceptable price to pay, even for the world's most important reserve currency.

As expected, inflation followed. By 1965, the gold value of the dollar was unchanged at 1/35 of an ounce, yet its purchasing power had decreased to 57% of 1945 levels. Not unrelated, Treasury gold reserves fell from $20.08 billion to just $13.80 billion, or less than 69% of 1945 levels. After only 21 years, the Bretton Woods system—along with the gold-backed American dollar—was melting. On February 18, 1965, Congress once again amended the Federal Reserve Act to eliminate all gold reserve requirements against deposits, then completed the process a few years later on March 18, 1968 by eliminating all gold reserve requirements against Federal Reserve notes. The American dollar was now a fiat currency, with no official backing of any hard asset.

The United States had tried desperately to prevent this from happening. As early as 1960, the world market price for gold had traded well above the official price, at one point reaching $40 per troy ounce. In November 1961, the U.S. Treasury had joined together with the Bank of England and the central banks of six major European nations to form a "gold pool," in an effort to maintain a stable official price by suppressing upward market pressures with coordinated gold sales. By 1968, the effort was deemed hopeless, and the gold pool was disbanded. This was coincident with the removal of all gold backing from Federal Reserve notes, and represented capitulation to the free market. For the next three years, gold traded in a two-tier market: one for official government transactions at the fixed price of $35, and one for private transactions at a higher, but variable, market price.

ABANDONMENT OF THE GOLD STANDARD

By 1969, the inflation rate in the United States had reached over 5%, with the blame most commonly placed on the costs of the Vietnam War and Lyndon Johnson's Great Society programs. Coupled with a rising balance of payments deficit, particularly with Japan, further downward pressure on the dollar was assured, as evidenced by the ever-rising price of gold.

The two-tier price system for gold was unworkable from the start. Once all gold backing for the circulating notes was removed, there was little reason to believe the United States could honor a fixed gold exchange rate with other nations for very long. Without a massive devaluation of the dollar, there was not enough gold in Fort Knox to cover all outstanding foreign obligations. More immediately, there was nothing to prevent a rogue nation from demanding gold from the Treasury at $35 and selling it on the open market at a higher price, turning a simple arbitrage transaction into an economic weapon. By the summer of 1971, President Nixon and Treasury Secretary John Connally saw the danger, and took unprecedented action.

On August 15, Nixon went on prime time national television to announce, "I have directed Secretary Connally to suspend temporarily the convertibility of the dollar into gold." The President's directive was subsequently described by apologists as a "closing of the gold window." A more accurate, albeit harsher assessment would have been an abandonment of the gold standard, a repudiation of the Bretton Woods agreement, and a debasement of the world reserve currency. Calling the decision "temporary" was as misleading as if Eisenhower had claimed he would temporarily occupy the beach at Normandy. The decision was irreversible, and the outcome uncertain. To quote Dr. Kwasi Kwarteng, "It was Nixon's decision in August 1971 which substantially altered the course of monetary history and inaugurated a period, for the first time in 2,500 years, in which gold was effectively demonetized in most of what had been understood to be the Western world" (214).

For the next four months after President Nixon's directive, the international currency markets operated without any formal structure or guidance. Fixed exchange rates were shelved, and the value of the dollar sank rapidly, losing more than 12% against both the German mark and the Japanese yen. World leaders convened in Washington to hammer out a new basis for monetary cooperation and stability.

On December 18, 1971, the President announced the Smithsonian Agreement, which revalued gold at $38 but failed to restore gold-dollar convertibility. The intent was to reintroduce fixed exchange rates by agreement only, without the discipline of actual gold transactions. The price of gold would be a yardstick, but physical gold would not change hands. Nixon called this "the greatest monetary agreement in the history of the world," but in fact, it was a product of wishful thinking, with no means of enforcement. Just 14 months later, in February 1973, the price of gold had to be officially raised once more, this time to $42.22 per ounce. By now, the charade was over: the "official" price of gold was meaningless. Within less than a year, the market price of gold tripled to $127.

The United States could no longer artificially overvalue the dollar in terms of gold and the currencies of its major trading partners. The ad hoc floating exchange rate system, supposedly adopted as a temporary response to Nixon's August 15 directive, was now permanent.

REPEAL OF THE GOLD LAWS

As previously detailed, United States monetary policy over a ten-year period went from gold market manipulation, to elimination of a gold-backed currency, to devaluation of the dollar, and ultimately to abandonment of the gold standard. Though dramatic, the immediate effects of these actions were primarily external. Unlike Roosevelt's national emergency, where bank closings and financial panic were experienced by the general public, the immediate disruptions caused by policies under Johnson and Nixon were in the foreign exchange markets, and not felt by most citizens until the rampant inflation of the 1970s set in. Nonetheless, the effects on world commerce were greater than anything since World War II. Businesses worldwide now had to deal with the uncertainties of constantly-shifting currency valuations, and the implications for foreign investment and banking strategies could fill a book all on their own.

Throughout this entire episode, Roosevelt's gold laws remained in place. They had no material effect, positive or negative, on the monetary instability of the 1960s and 70s, and whatever legal justification they may have once had—as detailed by Roosevelt himself in January 1934—was clearly no longer relevant. Since the repudiation of the gold standard, gold had become just a commodity, with no direct link to money. Any Constitutional authority to "coin money, and regulate the value thereof" no longer applied; thus, neither did its status as contraband. Gold was now just expensive property, no different from precious gems or fine art, and there was no compelling public interest in its prohibition or regulation. The only thing left for government to do was reverse their mistake.

On August 14, 1974, Congress passed public law 93-373 as follows:

> No provision of any law in effect on the date of enactment of this act, and no rule, regulation or order in effect on the date [this act] becomes effective may be construed to prohibit any person from purchasing, holding, selling, or otherwise dealing with gold in the United States or abroad.

With this change in place, there were two things left to do in order to completely reverse the legacy of Roosevelt's gold laws. First, the federal bureaucracy created to enforce those laws had to be dismantled. On December 31, 1974—the same day that the act officially took effect—President Ford signed Executive Order 11825 revoking all previous executive orders "pertaining to the regulations of the acquisition of, holding of, or other transactions in gold." Seven months later, Treasury Secretary William Simon ordered the Office of Domestic Gold and Silver Operations to be "disestablished and its functions terminated." The power of the state to control gold ownership was now physically, as well as legally, relinquished.

Second, the legal right to contract for payment in gold—that is, reestablishment of the gold clause as prohibited by the Joint Resolution of June 5, 1933, and later upheld by the Supreme Court in 1935—was not covered by the new law, and had to be addressed. The first attempt came in June 1975, but was rejected by Treasury Secretary Simon with the argument that payment in gold was still using gold as money. (The counterargument, of course, was that gold as property could be used as barter.) A year later, Senator Jesse Helms again offered similar legislation on the floor of the Senate, with assurances that re-legalization would not apply retroactively to gold contracts previously nullified, only to those entered into from that point forward. Senator Helms's legislation became law on October 28, 1977. After more than 40 years, Roosevelt's gold laws were finally repealed in full.

LESSONS OF CONFISCATION

President Roosevelt's attitudes and opinions on private gold ownership, as noted in Part I, were never publicly revealed before his election. Whether those opinions were long-held, or directly formed in response to the Banking Crisis of 1933, was perhaps known only by his closest confidantes. In either case, it is the author's opinion that political acceptance of Roosevelt's gold policies was based on a fundamental misunderstanding of the dual role of gold as both money and property.

The regulation of money is enumerated in the Constitution by the phrase "the power to coin money." In modern times, this includes the power to print money, which presents an important analogy: manufacturing money using paper as a basic material does not imply that a sheaf of plain paper is money. Similarly, minting a gold coin does not imply that a lump of gold is money. Both paper and gold in their raw forms are property, with only the potential of being made into money.

This distinction is not simply academic. Unlike money, our laws governing property are founded in English common law. They are not enumerated in the Constitution, and not regulated by Congress. The regulation of money is centered around the collective, while property law is focused on the individual, and is upheld and protected by the courts. The principle becomes even more clear when borders are crossed: as money, a legal tender gold coin can be constitutionally regulated by the government, but when a coin is exported, it becomes simple property, since a foreign government has no legal obligation to honor its monetary status. In fact, it has always been common practice for countries to melt foreign coins, destroying their former monetary value and reducing them to mere property in the form of bullion.

Gold as money is a construct of politics, while gold as property is a natural occurrence. Gold becomes money when it is used as a basic material for a circulating coinage, and is merely property when it is found as natural ore, or fabricated into artwork, jewelry, or bars. Defining the value of a dollar as 1/35 of an ounce of gold does not make gold money—rather, it values the dollar in terms of a stable asset. The dollar itself is a unit of account, used to measure the value of everything else. Backing the dollar with gold is using gold as collateral property, not transforming gold into money. We can give our money an absolute value in terms of gold, but gold can never have a permanent value in terms of money. As history shows, all monetary units are eventually revalued or replaced, while gold is permanent, with a continuing value beyond the monetary policy of any one government.

By lumping gold certificates in with coins and bullion, Roosevelt's gold laws attempted to eliminate this distinction. All three were treated the same, despite the fact that gold certificates are only money, gold bullion is only property, and gold coins are both. Specifically, confiscation was justified as "necessary to protect the *currency* system of the United States" (emphasis added,) and by accepting this reasoning, the public and their elected officials tacitly agreed that all gold was money. Prior conditioning no doubt played a role: America's money was "as good as gold;" the American Treasury was "on a gold standard;" America's debts were "payable in gold coin;" the national emergency of 1933 was a "gold crisis" fueled by "unwarranted withdrawals of gold and currency." In the eyes of the public, money and gold were synonymous, despite their legal distinctions. Roosevelt's gold agenda was unquestionably bolstered by this confusion.

Contributing to the gold/money misunderstanding was the speed at which President Roosevelt was able to implement his agenda. Prior to Inauguration Day, the idea of gold confiscation was a political non-starter. No politician could have seriously raised the issue without intense public backlash. It was only coincidence that the financial system collapsed within days of the new president taking office, and outgoing President Hoover intentionally left it to Roosevelt to declare a bank holiday and deal with the crisis. Roosevelt's actions within the first few days had an effect similar to a declaration of war—the public was willing to rally around a new leader in ways that were never previously considered, including acceptance of harsh monetary controls. The rapid implementation of those controls was unprecedented—two days to declare a bank holiday, three more days to pass the Emergency Banking Act, one day to suspend the convertibility of the dollar into gold, 26 days to require delivery of gold to a Federal Reserve member bank, two months to abrogate the gold clause in all contracts, and less than three months beyond that to fully criminalize the simple ownership of gold coins and bullion.

Could this monetary agenda have been accomplished so hurriedly in any other political and economic environment? Did the public acquiesce to these measures in the belief that, as with war, the emergency was temporary, and a return to normalcy was imminent? Was the gold-as-property distinction too philosophical, when the situation required practicality? Most importantly, could the president have ended the crisis *without* resorting to confiscation?

Many tools were available that would have allowed President Roosevelt to regulate gold as money without infringing on property rights. These included the suspension of payment in gold, suspension of gold coin manufacture and distribution, suspension of gold export in both coin and bullion, demonetization of gold coins, suspension of the gold standard, and devaluation of the currency in terms of both gold and other currencies. All of these could have been implemented on a temporary or long-term basis, without the seizure of privately-held property. Even the abrogation of the gold clause, which was highly controversial because of the sums of money involved, was upheld by the Supreme Court as necessary for the solvency of the nation, and did not require confiscation.

Whether or not these tools alone would have been sufficient to accomplish monetary stability is unknowable, but a number of points are incontestable:

1.) The policy of confiscation was never fully debated in the legislature, or in any open public forum before implementation.

2.) With the passage of the Gold Reserve Act in 1934, the policy of confiscation was never again reviewed or voted upon by Congress until August 1974.

3.) No legal action against confiscation was ever heard or ruled upon by the Supreme Court.

4.) Lower court findings against criminalization of gold ownership were ignored by the Treasury Department.

5.) President Roosevelt freely admitted after the fact that one purpose of confiscation was to use the profit realized by the Treasury (after the revaluation of gold from $20.67 to $35) to finance New Deal expenditures not covered by taxes. He knew subsequent government actions would raise the price of gold, so he forcibly collected it from law-abiding citizens, then reaped the benefits.

All things considered, the episode was not a proud moment for our democratic institutions. It took 40 years for American lawmakers to correct a misguided policy, while the British government reversed a similar policy in one-tenth the time. Congress could have been more thoughtful about giving a new president such sweeping powers less than a week into his administration, and President Roosevelt could have been more forthcoming about the need to raise money to pay for his New Deal programs. Proponents of private gold ownership could have been more insistent on open debate, and more tenacious in their use of the court system. The legislatures in later years could have acknowledged that any national emergency existing in 1933 had long since passed. And, any of the presidents following Franklin D. Roosevelt could have reviewed the gold laws in the rest of the free world during their tenure, and asked themselves why our policies alone resembled those of third-world dictatorships.

PART III:

PROSPECTS FOR GOLD

III.

WORLD MARKETS SINCE LEGALIZATION

When President Nixon "closed the gold window" in 1971, foreign exchange markets were thrown into chaos, and an unofficial system of floating exchange rates temporarily emerged. Efforts to reestablish a permanent system of fixed rates at the Smithsonian Conference failed after only a few months, and by February 1973, the idea of fixed exchange rates linked to a controlled price of gold was finally discredited and replaced with market-based valuations for both currencies and gold. To quote Paul and Lehrman, "Floating rates had not really been adopted; rather, fixed rates had been abandoned" (137).

In the nine years following Nixon's order to suspend payments in gold, the exchange rate of the dollar lost 50% against the German mark, 30% against the Japanese yen, and 60% against the Swiss franc. The inflation rate reached a high of over 12% in 1980, and the price of gold soared above $800, more than 22 times the official price of $35 under Bretton Woods. It is no exaggeration to say that closing the gold window in 1971 led to a decade of turmoil in the gold and currency markets. In the very middle of this turmoil, the United States legalized the private ownership of gold.

The markets eventually settled, and the 1980s provided a period of relative calm for world gold. Below is a chart of yearly gold prices for 1981 through 1990, based on daily London market price fixings in dollars.

Year	High Price	Low Price	Avg Price
1981	599	391	460
1982	488	296	375
1983	511	274	423
1984	406	303	360
1985	340	284	317
1986	442	326	368
1987	502	390	446
1988	485	389	436
1989	417	358	381
1990	423	345	382

With the price of gold remaining more or less stable during the decade of the 80s, the number of gold products offered to the American public for investment purposes grew rapidly. In 1967, South Africa was the first country to issue a mass-marketed gold coin based on weight, with no tie to a previous gold standard like the Austrian 100 corona or the Mexican 50 peso. Although illegal at first in the United States, the South African krugerrand was truly a product ahead of its time. It provided a way to invest in gold that made calculation of actual market value in any currency a simple matter. Each coin contained exactly one troy ounce of pure gold, the standard weight in which daily London gold prices were quoted. When gold was legalized in the United States after 1975, the floodgates were opened for new government-issued gold coins imitating the South African model, including:

Country	One-Ounce Gold Coin	Year of Issue
Canada	Maple Leaf	1979
China	Panda	1982
Australia	Nugget, Kangaroo	1986
United States	Gold Eagle	1986
Great Britain	Britannia	1987
Austria	Philharmonic	1989

In addition to government issues, private mints were also offering investment products, like the one-ounce Isle of Man Angel from the Pobjoy Mint in Britain. The Wall Street Journal joined the discussion with a May 5, 1987 article titled "New Glitter – Gold Finally Becomes a Respectable Holding for Investors in U.S." Taking note of the growing interest among smaller investors, the article concluded, "perhaps the most significant development in the U.S. gold market has been the American Eagle… The Eagle program has, in effect, put the government's stamp of approval on owning gold."

For the next two decades beginning in 1990, the most important developments in private gold ownership occurred outside the United States. With the fall of the Soviet Union, many new countries were created, including a restructured Russia, Belarus, Ukraine, Lithuania, Latvia, and Estonia, all of which eventually legalized gold and issued official gold coins of their own. In addition, the former Soviet bloc countries of Poland, Romania, and Hungary were freed from Soviet control, and Yugoslavia and Czechoslovakia were broken up into a number of free and independent nations. All of these countries joined the former soviet republics in eventually legalizing gold ownership.

The major event in Asia affecting the private ownership of gold was the transfer of Hong Kong to Chinese control in 1997. Many Hong Kong investors were afraid of a communist crackdown on Hong Kong's capitalist markets, but the actual result was a case of the tail wagging the dog. Over the next ten years, China slowly adopted many of Hong Kong's free market ideas, and restrictions on gold were ignored or lifted, including those on the early gold pandas, which were originally made for export only and prohibited to Chinese residents. Today, the Chinese markets for gold coins and gold bullion are some of the most active in the world.

While there is no causal link between legalization of gold in the United States and legalization in the rest of the world, the rapid pace of change is apparent. The freedom to own gold has spread worldwide to the point that it is now a recognized property right in all but the most repressive regimes. (Both Cuba and North Korea make gold coins for export, but residents never get to own them.) Once granted, the legal right to own gold is difficult to reverse, since private ownership is decentralized and no longer part of a circulating currency. Nonetheless, many Americans hold the belief that the threat of confiscation continues to exist, and that Roosevelt's policies could be resurrected at any time.

The first two parts of this book provided a historical review of gold confiscation, hopefully with a minimum of opinion and bias. In discussing this topic with friends, many asked the obvious question: "Can it happen again?" The final section offers a combination of personal opinion and contemporary observation in an attempt to answer that question, and provide a likely scenario for the future of gold ownership. My personal experience as a full-time coin dealer from 1976 to 2016 is the basis for my conceit in claiming a crystal ball that is better than most. I not only witnessed the momentous events of this period, but in many ways was a party to them. I would like to believe my experience and opinions will be of value to others.

GOLD TODAY – MONEY OR NOT?

This book has spent a great deal of time stressing the difference between gold as money and gold as property. Confiscation was made possible in part by the role of gold in our monetary system: it was used by the public as coinage, as well as by the Treasury to settle international account balances. Today, however, neither of these conditions exist. Gold has been legally demonetized, and the dollar has been reduced to a fiat currency.

So, is gold still money? Gold continues to serve as a reliable store of value, one of the primary functions of money. The treasuries of all economically-important countries still hold significant quantities of gold, even though it no longer serves a legal monetary purpose. However, trust in gold as an asset is not the same as equating gold with money. Gold fails any basic monetary test on two other points as well. First, it is no longer used as a generally accepted means of payment, and second, it does not serve as a unit of account for either business or government.

Even so, there are arguments in favor of gold as money that may not be legal, but are otherwise compelling. Gold is the most demanded commodity for trade or barter; gold is the asset most easily converted to any recognized currency; gold has a 2,500 year history superior to any fiat currency past or present; gold is a product of nature that is hard to extract and has confounded alchemists, while paper money is a product of government and can be corrupted at any time. Electronic money, the modern successor to paper money, is no different in this regard, other than being cheaper to produce and easier to track.

Legally, gold may not be money, but situations can arise where law no longer applies. Gold becomes money whenever it is generally accepted by the public as a superior form of payment to a failing currency, as with the Russian ruble in 1918, the German mark in 1923, or many European currencies following World War II. Gold is money by default when public confidence in paper money collapses. As long as gold is not part of an international monetary agreement, it will remain money-in-waiting, always available as an alternative to a failed monetary experiment.

Can a next-best-replacement for fiat currency qualify as money in the absence of any legal status? The issue is a matter of semantics, not substance. To a lawyer or a Treasury official, "demonetized" means it is not money, end of discussion. To others, a government's declaration plays no role in objective reality. The disagreement is not economic or financial, but political and philosophical. Gold is an emotional subject, involving freedom and independence, power and authority, and most of all, trust. So-called "gold

bugs" will always consider gold as the only money that governments can't corrupt, and gold bashers will always look down upon
it as a barbaric metal. Changing minds so entrenched is difficult, if
not impossible.

GOLD TODAY – INVESTMENT OR NOT?

An investment is an expenditure with two objectives. First, and
most importantly, is a complete return of the principle. Second is a
profit, in the form of interest, dividends, rent, or capital gains.
Since gold does not yield interest or dividends, the opportunity for
profit is limited to capital gains. (The possibility of rent or lease
income from gold does, in fact, exist, but it is a special circum-
stance within the securities industry and is unavailable to the average gold owner.)

Any assertion that gold cannot be an investment because it
yields no interest or dividends ignores the many accepted forms of
investment with the same limitations, including rare art, precious
stones, and historical artifacts. Arguing that investment in gold en-
tails no risk of failure neglects the obvious risk of capital loss, and
discounts all investments in commodities not subject to spoilage.
As long as the price of gold is left to the free market, not manipulated or controlled by government, the possibility of capital gain or
capital loss is sufficient to recognize gold as a valid form of investment. The fact that profiting from this investment is speculative
rather than contractual may bother some Wall Street conservatives,

but is irrelevant. After all, initial investment in Uber and Facebook was speculative, while General Motors bonds and Enron stock were thought to be conservative.

The two choices for direct investment in gold are physical gold, such as coins or bars, and gold securities such as exchange traded funds, futures contracts, and options contracts. Gold securities, often called paper gold, are legally complex and highly regulated by the federal government. By contrast, physical gold is easy to acquire, and relatively unregulated. Securities can be a preferred way to invest in gold when considering storage and transportation, transaction fees and taxes, and rapid access to efficient markets; they are also traded on centralized exchanges, monitored by numerous government agencies, and highly exposed to any attempt at restricting ownership or confiscating holdings. People who have no fear of these possibilities will feel comfortable owning gold in the form of securities. Physical gold will always be preferred by those who view it not only as an investment, but also as an insurance policy against government misdeeds. Those who scorn this way of thinking as conspiracy theory should consider that purchasing life insurance does not necessarily indicate an irrational fear of death, only acceptance of its inevitability. History demonstrates that gradual mismanagement and ultimate corruption of all fiat currencies is inevitable. The only unknown is in whose lifetime.

This final section addresses the prospects for gold and the possibilities of another attempt at confiscation. A full discussion of the present-day securities market would be well beyond the scope of this work, so the remainder of the text will concentrate on the private ownership of physical gold, and the possibilities for future regulation, taxation, restriction, and confiscation.

MARKETS FOR PHYSICAL GOLD

When gold coins commonly circulated as currency, there was no independent retail market for bullion gold. A $20 gold piece contained exactly $20 in bullion, based on the officially-controlled price of gold. When exchanging paper money for gold coins at a bank, there were no transaction fees or service charges. In effect, banks were selling bullion at cost. There was no business opportunity for an independent dealer to earn a profit.

When gold was legalized in 1975, only South Africa was mass-producing gold coins and marketing them to the public. Mexico and a few other countries still made restrikes of their pre-1933 coinage, but only the krugerrand was aggressively marketed as an investment. The retail outlets available for distribution of bullion products were limited to local coin shops and small independent coin dealers. The major banks in America had no experience or interest in marketing gold, and brokerage firms viewed gold as a foolish investment compared to stocks and bonds. No one in the corporate world stepped up to market gold to the public, so the opportunity was passed to the small merchant and individual entrepreneur.

Between 1975 and 1980, prices for precious metals surged, and small family-owned hobby shops selling stamps and coins to collectors on Saturday morning were transformed into investment-oriented gold and silver exchanges. Old class rings, sterling silver flatware, and unwanted jewelry were all purchased by weight, and everything was sold as scrap to smelters and refiners. Silver coins from 1964 and earlier were traded in thousand-dollar bags, and local coin shows were overpowered by the constant clatter of coin counting machines. California forty-niners used a pick and shovel to find gold; in 1980, shopkeepers just hung out signs reading "We Buy Gold and Silver" and saw it delivered to them hand over fist.

As with all gold rushes, the boom ended with a bust. Between 1980 and 1982, gold fell 65% to under $300, and silver fell an astonishing 90% to under $5. Coin shop profits evaporated, and most of the "We Buy" signs disappeared. Many of those who profited from the boom gave it all back (in every foolish way possible,) but the ones who managed their money wisely came away with two important assets: a battle-tested knowledge of the precious metals markets, and enough accumulated capital to stay in the retail gold business. Not only did the fittest survive, they emerged stronger than ever. The gold and silver boom of 1980 provided the initial financing for the network of gold dealers and retailers that exists today, and many if not most of these businesses are still owned and operated by the original founders and their children.

The modern manufacture of bullion products is highly centralized and dominated by nation states, including the U.S., China,

Australia, Canada, and Austria, but except for a very few licensed primary dealers, the retail distribution of these products is managed by small- and medium-sized businesses across the country. Banks, brokerage houses, and other traditional financial institutions have not participated at the retail level, opting to sell paper gold securities in lieu of physical gold. The most important segment of the bullion market, however, is not distribution of new product, but the purchase and resale of existing product from the public. This is exclusively a local or regional function, and accounts for the large majority of retail transactions. Buying, not selling, determines the relative success of a coin shop or precious metals exchange. Unlike jewelry stores, coin stores have not been successfully franchised because of the primary importance of buying.

The government, on the other hand, operates a one-way market for its products. They sell, but never buy. When the price of gold was fixed, the Treasury was forced to operate an "open window," and support the official price with a two-way market. Now that the window is closed and the price of gold is variable, there are no pressures on the government to buy or sell. They simply adjust the prices of all their gold products.

There is no public or private centralized market for the purchase of physical gold. It would in theory be possible for the government to group small coin shops together with pawn shops and regulate them as lenders, but so far, this is not a national issue. Unless the large banks—or retailers like Wal-Mart, with outlets in every community—begin offering nationwide purchasing of bullion gold, the retail market for gold coins, bars, and medals will remain decentralized and operated by independent dealers.

Along with decentralization, the other characteristic of the physical gold market that stands out is its limited regulation. Unlike banks and brokerage houses, coin shops and bullion dealers are not licensed and regulated as financial institutions by the federal government, and bullion products are not regulated by the Securities Exchange Commission as investments. The only significant federal regulations affecting coin dealers are cash reporting requirements.

Cash reporting is of particular importance to the Internal Revenue Service (due to potential tax evasion,) Homeland Security (terrorism funding,) and the Drug Enforcement Agency (money laundering.) The basic rule is that any cash transaction over $10,000 must be reported. While this requirement is easy enough to follow, difficulties arise from two amendments to the basic rule. The first is the notion of "structuring," defined by the IRS as limiting individual transactions to below $10,000 with the specific intent of evading the law. Identifying this offense places a coin dealer in the untenable position of being a mind reader—if a customer wants to purchase $9,000 worth of gold, how is the dealer supposed to know if the customer is "structuring" across multiple dealers, or simply spending all of his allocated funds?

The second amendment to the basic rule is the expanded definition of a $10,000 purchase to include "cumulative" cash purchases over one year. The meaning of cumulative creates as much uncertainty as the identification of intentional structuring. The cash purchases by a single customer of $2,000, $5,000, and $4,000 over less than 12 months clearly qualifies as a "cumulative" purchase, and is subject to reporting. But what if these purchases are separately undertaken by the wife, son, and brother of the customer? Is this simply a family with shared interests, or a cumulative purchase in disguise—or, for that matter, does it count as a form of structuring? Which records and forms are required? Could the dealer be criminally liable? Both structuring and cumulative purchases are offenses involving government discretion and selective enforcement, not clear-cut rules and norms.

Because of these uncertainties, along with the added paperwork, large bullion dealers and auction houses often refuse cash payment. Smaller dealers appealing to a walk-in trade are obliged to accept a certain amount of cash, but must be very careful in their record-keeping. Once the cash reporting laws and the possible traps are fully understood, however, most dealers accept compliance as a necessary annoyance. Overall, the regulation of the physical gold market in the United States is minimal. Whether it will remain so is a subject for later discussion.

MODERN MARKETING METHODS

While the market for physical gold remains decentralized and mostly unregulated, marketing methods have evolved with technology, expanding the geographic reach of small- and medium-sized dealers beyond anything imaginable in 1975. Local coin shops and coin shows are still important to the trade, but cable television and the internet now provide a national audience for firms previously limited to telephone, catalog, or in-person contact. Daytime business channels are flooded with 60-second spots touting gold as the ultimate investment, and 30-minute infomercials offering modern coin bargains are commonplace on late-night channels. But nothing has changed the coin and bullion business more in the last 10 years than the internet. Businesses of any size can now develop tremendous exposure for much less money than TV or print ads, using individual websites or any number of commercial auction platforms. Every young dealer trying to build a coin business in today's market is relying on the internet for initial success.

Coin and bullion dealers have traditionally depended on personal contact and customer trust more than retailers of consumer goods do. The amount of money involved and the opportunity for fraud or theft demand a relationship between dealer and customer that is more fiduciary than commercial. A big problem with gold transactions initiated on cable TV or the internet is overcoming the lack of trust that inherently exists between strangers. In the fields of banking, securities, or real estate, the government acts as an unseen participant to all transactions by providing rules, regulations, and penalties—the function of a referee. In the coin and bullion business, there are few government regulations, so it was left to the free market to invent products and services that could establish trust between dealers and customers who were unknown to one another.

In the 1980s, a number of private organizations began offering authentication and grading services for coins and medals. Earlier products consisted of a certificate with a photograph, but newer firms experimented with tamper-resistant plastic holders. The idea was first introduced in South Africa as a way to promote proof krugerrands. Benefits over a photo-certificate included physical protection, ease of handling, and conjoining of coin with professional opinion. The South Africans understood that encapsulation was not necessarily for the benefit of the present owner, but rather for future owners—in other words, a means of facilitating trade. Combining a professional opinion with a convenient holder could insert a measure of objectivity between strangers doing business.

When certified coins in plastic holders, also known as "slabs," first appeared on the American market, there was no such thing as the internet as we know it today. A network did exist, but generally speaking it was not yet exploited for commercial purposes. The strategy behind certification was to make coins fungible—or interchangeable, like shares of stock—in the hopes of attracting investors more comfortable with commodities than unique and illiquid works of art. Initially, Wall Street bought the idea, and a few of the largest brokerage firms promoted limited partnerships with the purpose of owning and trading "an investment-quality portfolio" of certified coins. As it turned out, these funds were a bust for a number of reasons (some embarrassing and never fully disclosed,) and Wall Street abandoned the experiment. At the time, there was no way of predicting that the internet, rather than Wall Street, would make certification a veritable utility within the coin business by providing third-party objectivity and trust to transactions between strangers.

Today, it is difficult to sell any coins of significant value on TV, at auction, or over the internet without certification. Both buyer and seller benefit from this development. Buyers rely on certification to shelter them from misrepresentation, and sellers need certification to protect against legal liability. Both sides welcome the participation of a referee, and commerce is stimulated without government or Wall Street intervention.

Now comes the difficult and dubious task of predicting the future and assessing the possibility of another Roosevelt-style confiscation of gold. The rest of the discussion is divided into three topics: market trends, monetary trends, and legal trends. The future of private gold ownership will depend on all three.

MARKET TRENDS

When President Roosevelt issued his April 5, 1933 executive order forbidding the hoarding of gold coins, he made a specific point distinguishing numismatic gold from common circulating gold. By exempting "gold coins having a recognized special value to collectors of rare and unusual coins," Roosevelt sought to establish a legal wall between coins found in museums, and coins carried in pockets or handbags. (He saw no need, on the other hand, to differentiate between gold coins as money and as property.) By using the constitutional power to regulate money, he could effectively seize most of the gold bullion held by the public.

Today, however, there are no circulating gold coins, and gold is no longer legal money. Roosevelt's distinction between numismatic gold and circulating gold is obsolete. The new dichotomy is between numismatic gold and bullion gold. With the exception of commemorative issues, modern gold coins are all minted as bullion and carry a meaningless face value. Is it possible, or even desirable, to legally distinguish them from collector coins?

Many gold investors collect one-ounce bullion coins by date or type, and many bullion coins made specifically for the investor market are slabbed by promoters to appeal to collectors. From the other point of view, many collectors only buy coins close to bullion value, and many certified collector coins are eventually sold for bullion and sent to the refinery. Is a Chinese panda or a "low mintage" American eagle a collectible, or merely bullion? Any attempt to devise a legal distinction between the two seems like folly. Today's markets for bullion gold and numismatic gold overlap by at least 30%, in my experience.

Roosevelt could confiscate gold because it was money, and exempt coins as numismatic if they had a market value greater than face value. Circulating gold was money, and numismatic gold was private property. Today, however, bullion gold and numismatic gold are both property, and differentiating the two would have to be based solely on property value. I believe any effort to exclude numismatic items from future gold restrictions or regulations would have to define collectibles as having a market value substantially over bullion value, perhaps as high as 50% to 100%. The great majority of gold coins currently traded as collectibles in the secondary market would have to be disallowed, including most pre-1933 U.S. issues. Only significant collections of true museum quality could be exempted from future gold restrictions, if they were to have any impact.

There are three dominant trends guiding today's markets for gold coins and gold bullion. First, the internet has been a disruptive factor, and its importance continues to grow. The financial sector uses the term "disintermediation," which is a fancy way of describing the elimination of the middle man. Coin and bullion dealers are all middlemen, and, like stockbrokers, are subject to replacement by electronic trading platforms. Professional advice from a human is not always needed.

Second, coin collecting as a hobby is fading. Membership in the American Numismatic Association, the premier national organization for coin collectors, fell over 22% between 2007 and 2017. Getting people under 30 interested in coin collecting is becoming increasingly difficult, since young people today prefer cards to cash and don't carry pocket change. The government has introduced commemorative coin programs such as state quarters and presidential dollars to stimulate collecting, but quarters can't compete with smartphones for juvenile attention, and dollar coins end up as vault cash at the various Federal Reserve depositories. Simply stated, there are not enough young enthusiasts to replace those leaving the hobby due to age, or loss of interest. The ANA is working hard to reverse this trend, but the only solution may be to broaden the base by including more collectors of tokens, medals, scrip, books, documents, and other Americana.

The third major trend affecting the coin business is the aging of the collecting community. The average age of an ANA member today is 61. A common topic among dealers at every major coin convention is who will be left in ten years. I started my career at 28, and most of the dealers I know are still Baby Boomers just like me. Unless the demographics of the hobby change considerably, coin shows of the future may look like shuffleboard courts in Florida.

These three trends are certain to continue, and will all have a significant impact on the gold bullion markets of the future. My estimate of their effects on particular market segments is detailed below. In making these predictions, I have given due consideration to Dennis Miller's trademark quote, "that's just my opinion; I could be wrong."

1.) Coin Shops – The local coin shop offering a wide selection of numismatic coins and supplies to collectors is rapidly disappearing, and like stamp shops, will be completely gone in the coming years. Existing stores are largely dependent on gold and silver bullion transactions to stay in business, and many dealers have traded their storefront location for less expensive office space. Long before the gold and silver boom of 1980, New York City had a vibrant coin district with dozens of shops in the vicinity of 45th Street and 6th Avenue. Today, an independent retail coin shop in midtown Manhattan would have a hard time covering the rent, much less turning a profit. Collector coins by themselves can no longer support a storefront; they must be subsidized by trading in bullion, jewelry, diamonds, watches, or other collectibles. In the future, the term "coin shop" will refer to bullion coins, with numismatics a minor consideration. Collector coins purchased across the counter will be wholesaled to other dealers, or marketed through other channels.

2.) Coin shows – The coin and bullion business has no large, permanently-situated exchange facility or trade district like the one located in New York during the 1950s and 1960s. The only semblance of an organized national marketplace in the last 40 years has been a collection of independent regional and national coin conventions. Taken together, they form a commercial circuit for the coin business. Dealers and customers periodically gather in hotels and convention centers across the nation to engage in trade and settle accounts. While the sponsors of a coin convention always emphasize the educational and fraternal benefits, the fundamental attraction for any show is access to fresh dealer inventory. For both dealer and collector, "going to market" means attending a major numismatic convention.

Coin shows of the future face two significant headwinds, both involving the internet. First, the amount of new material being offered at shows is decreasing. Dealers are diverting recent purchases to company websites and internet auctions in the hopes of reaching a broader audience. Second, many would-be show attendees are avoiding hotel and airfare expenses by shopping online. With fewer coins to choose from and rising travel costs, the decision to shop at home is becoming easier.

Coin shows are not in danger of disappearing, but are certainly in the process of downsizing. The human advantages of a coin show, including sight-seen evaluation, in-person negotiation, live market exposure, and common interest social interaction can never be offered by the internet, but dealer participation, customer foot traffic, and overall quality of material on display are all in decline. Dealers and collectors are aging out, high-dollar items are going to auction, and sales are increasingly dependent on bullion items and modern mint issues. Any rarities on display are often grossly over-priced, or not for sale. Coin shows are becoming less a commercial event, and more a social event.

3.) Auction Firms – While the internet has been disruptive to coin shops and coin shows, its effect on the auction business has been transformative. In the 1980s, a major coin auction would have 50-100 active floor bidders, sometimes more. Most were dealers, buying either for specific customers on commission or for their own account, and most winning bids came from the floor. Success-ful telephone or mail bidders were a minority. When a lot did go "to the book," it was often a reserve bid by the owner.

Today, a coin auction with floor bidding is often attended by as few as 10 people, and almost all successful bids are submitted via the internet—many in real time. Every major auction house claims thousands of active online bidders from all over the world, and with drastically-increased bidder participation, the prices realized have often been astounding. Many dealers competing for the same lots claim that internet bidders pay "too much," because their bidding is more emotional than rational. My own belief is that outcomes are statistical, and greater participation brings greater knowledge but also greater error. Some lots are sold to the highest mistake. But no matter what the cause, higher prices realized have brought a significant increase in auction consignments. The worldwide exposure provided by digital technology greatly enhances the prospect of finding the ultimate buyer for any rare and valuable item. The old model of floor bidding at auction is going the way of open pit trading on the stock exchanges. Both have become largely ceremonial, and are soon to become extinct.

4.) Internet Marketing – The widespread use of websites and internet auction platforms within the coin and bullion business is well known, and there is ample reason to believe that this type of marketing will increase in the near future. The many advantages—including low overhead, minimal barriers to entry, and limited regulation and taxation—make internet marketing an easy choice for both startup and expansion. Many companies use the internet as a complimentary marketing strategy to an existing coin shop, coin show, or office-based operation. An internet presence can be of benefit to any size firm, from a part-time sole proprietorship to the largest coin and bullion trader.

5.) Mass Marketing – Internet marketing centers on a potential customer initiating a search for specific product or merchant. The customer already has a good idea of what he wants, and direct contact with a sales representative is often bypassed entirely. This is very different from mass marketing, where the merchant initiates the search, looking for new customer "leads," and follows up with personal contact from a professional sales staff hired to close the sale. Internet marketing is passive, like a fisherman with rod and reel waiting for a bite. Mass marketing is active, like a fisherman with a spear gun.

Internet marketing of coins and bullion is highly decentralized, involving thousands of merchants of all sizes nationwide. By contrast, mass marketing involves very expensive advertising campaigns, and is dominated by relatively few big-budget firms. Mass marketers are high profile by design, and attract the attention of the Securities Exchange Commission and the Federal Communications Commission. Internet marketers are too numerous and too dispersed to justify similar attention. Future restrictions and regulations on the sale of gold coins and bullion will most likely be enforced on mass marketers first. A common government strategy is to focus enforcement on a single big player as a way of encouraging voluntary compliance from others. In my opinion, lower-profile dealers will not be specially targeted by any future gold regulations. Their cooperation will be assumed.

Government restrictions are often dependent on commercial chokepoints for enforcement. The chokepoints for customs compliance are ports of entry, and the chokepoints for mandatory child vaccination are public schools. In 1933, President Roosevelt needed a chokepoint to confiscate gold from the public. Since most privately-owned gold was circulating money, the natural choice was the banking system. Under pressure from the Treasury and the

Federal Reserve, every bank in the United States was an accomplice to Roosevelt's confiscation.

Today, the banking system can no longer serve as a chokepoint for gold regulations of any kind. With gold demonetized, all privately-owned gold is either bullion, non-circulating legal tender, or numismatic coin. The reason for detailing the modern marketing channels for gold is to examine possible chokepoints that might be used to enforce any new government regulations.

The first chokepoint government would choose is the Federal Mint and its distribution network for new Mint products. Next would come control of all gold imports and exports, using Customs Bureau assets already in place. Both the Bureau of the Mint and the Customs Bureau are divisions of the Treasury, and could be mobilized quickly to manage and enforce any new gold regulations.

There would be major difficulties, however, with enforcement of restrictions involving gold already in the hands of the public. There are no natural chokepoints in today's markets for controlling the exchange or ownership of gold. Coin shops, coin shows, and internet marketers are all too unregulated and decentralized to provide the government with any enforcement leverage. Auction houses and mass marketers are generally larger and more regulated, but both are too few in number, and would most likely end up as victims rather than agents of enforcement. Without any viable chokepoints, government would have to rely on arbitrary prosecution or voluntary cooperation to enforce restrictions on gold. Considering that a primary reason for owning gold is lack of trust in

government and its management of a fiat currency, public cooperation with any effort to limit the freedom to own gold would most
likely be limited, if not trivial.

MONETARY TRENDS

The most significant monetary trend over the last 30 years has
been the rise in importance of currencies other than the dollar. In
1944, the Bretton Woods agreement created an international financial system based on two types of monetary reserves: gold, and a
gold-backed American dollar. The system remained intact until
1971, when President Nixon suspended gold-dollar convertibility,
and was dismantled entirely in 1973 when the International Monetary Fund (created by Bretton Woods) declared the agreement
dead, and dropped gold as a benchmark for currency valuation.
Even with this repudiation of gold, the dollar continued as the
most important reserve currency because of its widespread use in
world trade and finance. Natural resources and farm products were
almost all priced in dollars, and no other currency was abundant
enough to accommodate the volume of international transactions.

In the mid-1980s, other currencies began to challenge the su-
premacy of the dollar. The creation of the euro as a pan-European
currency and the growing strength of the Japanese yen were followed a decade later by the formidable rise of the Chinese yuan.
Today, pundits speculate on the future of the Indian rupee, the
Brazil real, and the Russian ruble, as well as a post-Brexit British

pound. How long the dollar can remain as the world's preeminent currency is a matter of geopolitical strategy, not just economic parlor talk.

The value of any currency is based on public confidence. Even a circulating bullion currency is based on the confidence that the coins are the full weight and specified fineness. Britain faced this challenge in 1695-1696, when it was forced to replace a heavily-clipped and lightweight-hammered coinage with newly-minted milled coins, which were full weight and protected from clipping. By agreeing to honor the old coins at full value for about four months, the Treasury suffered a great financial loss but retained public confidence in the money. Again in the 1880s, Britain realized that many of the circulating sovereigns and half-sovereigns were as much as 10% below standard weight due to normal wear, and in 1889, passed an Act of Parliament declaring that any loss of value should fall on the state, and not on the last user. Once again, Britain honored the nominal value of its circulating bullion coinage, and kept its promise of a true bullion-exchange currency. Confidence in the system was well-placed.

The dollar-gold exchange system established at Bretton Woods was founded on international confidence that the U.S. dollar would continue to be convertible to gold at $35 per ounce indefinitely. This confidence was broken in 1971, when Nixon closed the gold window.

Today, the American dollar is supported by international confidence that the U.S. government will honor its promises to repay debt and maintain stable cross-currency valuations. This ultimate confidence is circular self-deception: one fiat currency is valued in terms of other fiat currencies. There is no benchmark of value independent from politics. Is this confidence well-placed? With growing government debt, a highly-leveraged central bank, and massive unfunded social commitments, how long can this confidence last? Could a cataclysmic event force a new Bretton Woods-style paradigm? And would a change in the international status of the dollar prompt new restrictions on gold?

All considerations of the future involve a timeline with the status quo on the left, assumed events and decisions in the middle, and logical outcomes on the right. Thinking is left to right, starting with the present, and ending with a prediction. The probable accuracy of the prediction decreases as the number of assumptions increases. This model of thinking, while commonly used for routine decisions, is poorly-suited to problems as complex as the fate of the dollar, where the number of assumptions involved approaches infinity. The only productive approach to a problem this complex is to identify a finite array of possible outcomes, and work backwards—that is, to start with an outcome, and identify various events and decisions that could lead there. By limiting the number of outcomes, consideration of possible responses becomes manageable.

The future of the dollar as a world reserve currency (as opposed to merely a national currency) can be considered using three basic scenarios: long-term stability, peaceful evolution, and abrupt failure. A series of narratives leading to each scenario is offered below, followed by a discussion of how the private ownership of gold might be affected.

1.) Long-term Stability – Any narrative resulting in long-term stability for the dollar must begin with the premise that the Chinese yuan will continue to gain international stature, and that the euro could compete with the dollar by looking east for new trade relationships involving natural resources. The Chinese have maximized their manufacturing capabilities, and are relying on the consumer and financial sectors for a continued growth of 6%, compared to a projected American growth of just 3%. At these rates, the Chinese economy will double in 12 years, while the American economy grows less than 43% during the same period. Based on a gross national product that soon may be the largest in the world, massive foreign currency reserves, and a growing gold stock supplied by state-funded mining operations, the Chinese could soon pressure the International Monetary Fund for an equal seat at the table alongside the United States.

European currency, meanwhile, is facing a geopolitical shift from west to east, both economically and militarily. From the west, Britain is exiting the European Union, and the United States is demanding increased contributions from NATO partners for their collective security. From the east, Europe is increasingly dependent upon Russia for natural gas and oil, while remaining militarily complacent over Russian occupation of the Ukraine. It is logical for Europeans to look eastward for new trade agreements that exchange natural resources for technology, thus promoting both economic and military security. These overtures might also include Iran and China, and would put Europe in direct competition with Japan for long-term supplies of energy and raw materials. European cooperation with Russia would only enhance the international standing of the euro as a competitor to the dollar.

All of these trends suggest some form of long-term equilibrium between the dollar, the yuan, and the euro. The IMF would be a logical referee, with the three currencies having equal strength as a medium of international finance. Each currency might enjoy a particular sphere of influence based on geographic proximity and economic ties, with the stronger countries like Great Britain and Japan engaging freely with all three.

While the long-term stability outcome is certainly the most desirable, I do not rank it as the most probable. Expecting governments and central banks to act unselfishly is unrealistic—sooner or later, a competitive or nationalistic posture is inevitable. More importantly, the long-term stability scenario assumes no catastrophic event such as war, financial upheaval, or political collapse, any one of which could precipitate a different scenario.

2.) Peaceful Evolution – All narratives in this category begin with a significant financial disruption, and end with an international monetary solution, most likely provided by the IMF, in order to avoid war or social unrest. Previous disruptions have included closing the gold window in 1971, rampant dollar inflation circa 1980, and collapse of the mortgage bond market in 2008. In each of these cases, the International Monetary Fund provided the needed central bank liquidity to ease the crisis by issuing a "super currency" known as *special drawing rights*.

SDRs were created in 1969 and originally backed by the approximately 5,000 tons of gold held by the IMF. They were intended to temporarily augment the currency reserve positions of member countries during a crisis. In 1973, the gold backing was dropped, and replaced by a basket of currencies, all of which were fiat issues with floating market valuations. The basket remained mostly unchanged until 1999, when the euro replaced the German mark and the French franc. In 2016, the Chinese yuan was added. Today, the basket contains the following balance of currencies:

U.S. dollar	42%
European euro	31%
Chinese yuan	11%
Japanese yen	8%
British pound	8%

Three points need to be made regarding SDRs. First, they are not a currency. They are properly labeled "rights," and do not circulate anywhere except among central banks. Second, the IMF answers to no one, and can issue SDRs in any quantity and at any time. SDRs are a totally unregulated financial derivative that backstops the fiat currencies of the world. Third, the basket of currencies and their relative weighting can be changed at any time by the IMF members. This makes both the value and the use of SDRs a political decision as much as an economic one.

The peaceful evolution scenario assumes that financial disruptions will become more frequent in the future (a book-length topic in itself,) and that the use of SDRs will be required to the point that they become the primary world reserve currency. Evolution will take place with a gradual shift in the weightings of various basket currencies, in particular between the dollar and the yuan. Peaceful outcomes will be supported by the continued use of local currencies for international payments. Each currency will be traded in the financial markets against other major currencies, and whatever regulation is needed will be enforced by the IMF through control of SDRs. Interest rates could be managed by issuing debt instruments denominated in SDRs, and using them to expand reserves.

In this scenario, the IMF becomes the world's central banker, and SDRs become the permanent substitute for gold and the dollar as dictated by Bretton Woods. The SDR basket will continue to include the dollar, and gold could even be added as a component to the basket, but the primacy of the Federal Reserve and the dollar will be forever lost. America will be forced to manage its monetary reserves rather than print them. The world's central bank and lender of last resort will continue to be an authoritarian institution run by unelected bureaucrats—they just won't be our bureaucrats.

3.) Abrupt Failure – The first scenario depicts the dollar as both a world reserve currency, shared with the euro and yuan, and also a strong local or domestic currency. Scenario number two drops the dollar as a reserve currency, but maintains it as a local currency backed by IMF-issued special drawing rights. The last scenario envisions a dollar that not only loses its reserve currency status, but also loses the confidence of the American public as the most preferred form of money.

An abrupt failure of the dollar would be much more than a monetary event. It would very likely involve some combination of all-out war, societal breakdown, or financial market implosion. Gaming the causes and repercussions of these is well beyond my, or arguably anyone's, abilities. For our purposes here, it is sufficient to acknowledge that the risk exists.

In the past, wars and revolutions ended with local or regional monetary failure. The only true world currency, gold, might be squandered, stolen, or hidden, but it could never fail. Today, the entire world operates on fiat money, and a failure of the dollar would be a world failure. The complexity and interdependence of financial markets would guarantee a chain reaction much worse than the mortgage bond collapse of 2008.

The immediate world response, most likely headed by the IMF, would be another Bretton Woods-style conference, with the specific objective of creating a new circulating world currency. Unlike SDRs, the new currency would have to be available to the general population. Nation states would still be responsible for their own currencies, and the IMF currency would be supported by a weighted basket of these national currencies (that is, whichever ones survived.) It would also probably include some gold as a way of placating skeptics. The IMF would be the world's central bank, issue debt, and manage the new world currency the same way central banks operate today.

These three scenarios cover a wide range of narratives for the future of the dollar, from optimistic to pessimistic. They also suggest a continuum of government motivations for the increased regulation and possible confiscation of privately-owned gold: from indifference, to practical concern, to desperation.

The stability represented by the first scenario would prompt little change to current gold policies. Gold would remain legal to own, demonetized for transactions, and traded as a commodity on open markets. Any changes that did occur would likely include regulation of gold as a cash substitute in money laundering, terror finance, tax evasion, or other economic crimes. These would function more as extensions of current policy, rather than substantive changes.

The peaceful evolution scenario focuses on special drawing rights rising in status to primary reserve asset, replacing the dollar and other circulating currencies. The basket of currencies used to calculate the value of the SDR might be expanded to include gold, remonetizing the metal at an inflated value. In this instance, the government would most likely revisit all gold policies, in particular capital gains tax and sales reporting. Any rapid increase in the dollar value of gold would revive Roosevelt's 1934 assertion of "unjust enrichment."

The last scenario, abrupt failure of the dollar, would create a condition of desperation wherein any economic restriction might be justified under the guise of "national emergency." The exact wording of the Emergency Banking Act of 1933 already supports this assertion:

> Whenever in the judgment of the Secretary of the Treasury such action is necessary to protect the currency system of the United States, the Secretary of the Treasury, in his discretion, may require any or all individuals, partnerships, associations and corporations to pay and deliver to the Treasurer of the United States any or all gold coin, gold bullion, and gold certificates owned by such individuals, partnerships, associations or corporations.

Whether or not the country were at war, the government would treat an abrupt failure of the dollar as a wartime event. In this situation there would be few, if any, limitations on the revocation of property rights for purposes of national recovery. The low probability of this scenario does not exclude its mention.

LEGAL TRENDS

Legal action potentially affecting the private ownership of gold includes regulation, taxation, and confiscation. As covered earlier, current regulation of physical gold transactions is relatively low compared to regulation of the securities or banking industries. At the federal level, taxation of gold is consistent with other investment assets. At the state level, sales tax treatment varies considerably, with 35 states currently offering a full or partial exemption on coin and bullion purchases. Legal avoidance of state sales tax on gold is easily manageable with a little planning. Lastly, confiscation of gold has been a non-issue since 1975.

While the current legal environment for gold markets and gold ownership is generally benign, there is no reason to believe the situation is permanent. Any shift in the international status of the dollar could prompt changes in federal gold laws. Below is a discussion of possibilities, with no pretense of being exhaustive.

POTENTIAL REGULATION CHANGES

1.) Monetary Equivalent – Recent fears of money laundering associated with terrorism have led to many changes in the banking sector covering new accounts, international wire transfer, and foreign exchange. Gold could soon be declared a monetary equivalent, similar to money orders or traveler's checks, thus leading to regulation ordered by Homeland Security. The DEA and IRS also have an interest in gold as a disguised form of money transfer.

2.) Transaction Limitations – Just as cash transactions over $10,000 must be reported by banks and merchants, and the declaration by foreign travelers of large sums of cash must be made to customs officials, large transactions involving gold as payment could be made reportable, or possibly illegal, as evidence of intent to launder money.

3.) Import and Export Limitations – Imports and exports could be controlled by licensing, tariffs, or direct quotas. This is the most simple form of regulation, since the necessary assets are already in place at both the Customs Bureau and the Commerce Department.

4.) Dealer Licensing – Dealers in gold could be required to obtain a license from the Treasury or Homeland Security. Detailed recordkeeping would follow licensing, including evidence of sales, purchases, and customer identity. Background checks and financial bonding might also be required.

5.) Owner Registration – New account information, similar to that required of banks and stockbrokers, would be collected by all licensed dealers. All transactions would be shared with the IRS and other federal agencies. This would be the final step short of confiscation. The number of dealers would be greatly reduced. Coin shows would be renamed "hobby" shows, and flea markets would become black markets.

POTENTIAL TAX LAW CHANGES

1.) Enhanced Enforcement – This is probable under any economic scenario. Increased tracking of social media and web commerce will soon turn credit monitoring into economic profiling. Credit and data collection agencies will be forced to cooperate with federal authorities and provide information just as banks and phone companies currently do.

2.) Declaration of Gold Holdings – Similar to the declaration of all foreign bank accounts, gold holdings might become a required question on income tax returns.

3.) New Taxes – A federal transfer tax or excise tax on gold are both possible. In addition, any value-added tax (VAT) or national sales tax could include gold coins and gold bullion.

4.) Excess Profits Tax – In the event of an international revaluation of gold, a one-time tax might be assessed in the name of "unjust enrichment." This would be added to any capital gains tax on the books, and could conceivably be as high as 100%. With enough new taxes in place, direct confiscation might be considered unnecessary.

POSSIBLE CONFISCATION ACTIONS

Unless gold is remonetized internationally, any effort to confiscate privately-owned gold would most likely be presented as a form of eminent domain—that is, forced sale to the government at a "fair market value" in the best interests of the public at large. In this case, the following actions would be taken more or less simultaneously:

1.) An executive order would be issued for the surrender of all gold coins and gold bullion to licensed gold dealers at a fixed price. Dealers would be responsible for authentication and custody of the gold, pending delivery to an agent of the Treasury. Payment would be made directly by Treasury draft after a short verification and processing period.

2.) Manufacturing and distribution of all U.S. gold coins would cease. Coins already distributed would be recalled.

3.) Ports of entry would be sealed for all import and export of gold coins and bullion.

4.) Safe deposit boxes would be frozen, subject to bank inspection and inventory.

5.) Individual retirement accounts holding gold would be forced to liquidate.

6.) A government marketing campaign would promote the patriotic duty of cooperating with official orders in time of national emergency. An appeal would be made to purchase government bonds as a replacement for gold holdings. A return to normalcy in the near future would be assured, and the word propaganda would only be used with reference to our enemies.

CAN IT HAPPEN AGAIN?

Will the United States government ever again order the "surrender" of privately-owned gold? This is the gold bug's nightmare, and the immediate question a friend asked when I mentioned I was writing a book titled *Confiscation*. In only a few seconds, he identified the essence of the subject: fool me twice, shame on me.

The relevant question, however, is not "can it happen?," since the government obviously has the power, nor "will it happen?," because a bookmaker's odds are only of interest to a gambler. It is useless to know the odds of lightning striking an individual out for a walk, but quite useful to know of the particular danger lightning poses to a golfer swinging a metal club on an open fairway. Useful information offers a potential change in behavior. The questions that should be asked, therefore, are "why would the government want to confiscate gold?," and "what would be the warning signs?" The answers to these are both relevant, and actionable.

There are two compelling reasons for potential government confiscation of gold. First would be a dire need for hard money. This need is almost always the result of demands from external creditors who refuse payment in local currency. A government may force its own citizens to accept a fiat currency, but it cannot force foreign interests to do so, short of declaring war. A lack of hard currency leaves a government with three options: renege on the debt, earn the hard currency through trade, or take it from the citizenry by means of taxation or confiscation. (A fourth option, practiced by Nazi Germany during World War II, is to loot the gold of other countries through invasion or occupation. This is just confiscation at an international level.)

A second reason for gold confiscation would be a political desire for absolute control of the currency. Gold as money is beyond government control, because it cannot be created, only used. Absolute control of a national currency requires the ability to create money whenever needed, without restriction, and to outlaw the use of competitive currencies. Control is lost when confidence in the local currency is diminished, and alternative forms of payment for domestic transactions arise. Gold has traditionally been the preferred alternative to a failing currency, and confiscation would be one step toward regaining control.

While the motivations for confiscation in 1933 were basically the same as today, President Roosevelt had to deal with a very different monetary system. The United States was on a gold exchange standard, with gold freely exchangeable for paper dollars at a fixed price. When the newly-elected president was confronted with an unprecedented demand for gold in preference to paper, he had to stop the outflow of gold from the Treasury and modify the monetary system to restore balance. Since gold and money were synonymous, Roosevelt (or at least his highly-cooperative Congress) had the Constitutional authority to regulate both. He chose to regulate gold ownership first, and the gold exchange value of the dollar second. By proceeding in this order, he could claim any increase in the value of gold for the Treasury, as discussed in Part I. Whether this was an added motivation for confiscation, or merely the unintended consequence of a series of emergency measures, depends on one's political perspective.

Today, gold is not legal money. The value of the dollar is no longer tied to gold, and confidence in the dollar is no longer primarily dependent on the amount of gold in the Treasury. Any Constitutional argument for confiscation of gold as a form of monetary regulation would be much weaker than it was in 1933, and the threshold for government action would be much greater. President Roosevelt was able to surprise the populace with his gold policies by declaring an immediate need for monetary stability. Today, the connection between private gold ownership and monetary stability is tenuous at best. For both legal and logistical reasons, another surprise confiscation is implausible. A buildup to any major government action would be necessary, providing adequate warning signs.

The earliest warning signs for new gold regulations, including possible confiscation, would be wild swings in the markets for both gold and the dollar. Today, we take the availability of this information for granted, but in 1933 there were no publicly-traded markets for gold and currencies, and the numbers concerning financial supply and demand were generally kept within banking circles. Any gross imbalances in today's financial markets would be instantly revealed to the public, and spur public demand for government action.

A second category of warning sign would involve any change in the international financial structure, whether by agreement at the International Monetary Fund or in a new collaboration of world economic powers. Such changes could include any revisions to the basket of currencies supporting special drawing rights, or the creation of an entirely new world currency. In particular, the addition of gold as partial support for any international financial instrument would be a major warning sign. If gold is remonetized on an international level in any way, the Constitutional argument for regulation of gold as money will be reopened.

The third type of warning sign would be new government requirements and regulations on either the purchase or ownership of gold. In 1933, banks provided a national chokepoint for the confiscation of gold, since most privately-owned gold was in the form of coins that naturally flowed through the banking system for commercial purposes. Government-regulated banks were the contemporary "dealers" in gold, and could be directed to enforce any new gold regulations. Today, the dealer network for gold is both unregulated and highly decentralized, so it follows that the first step to confiscation would have to be the licensing of dealers, in order to establish the necessary chokepoints and gather data on ownership. *The licensing of coin dealers would be the most important warning sign to any future confiscation of gold.*

Other methods of gathering information on gold ownership could also be employed. The IRS already collects information on assets, as well as income. They know about retirement accounts, brokerage accounts, and real estate holdings. They currently require a declaration of foreign bank accounts as part of a normal tax return, and in the future this could be expanded to include all cash or cash-equivalent holdings, such as gold, or even cryptocurrencies like bitcoin. The effect would be a back door registration of gold owners that could be used for confiscation as well as taxation.

Until a federally-controlled dealer network is established and a federal database of gold ownership is compiled, any attempt at confiscation would be based purely on voluntary cooperation and doomed to failure. These activities, along with market fluctuations and financial changes on the international level, would provide the advance warning that was missing under Roosevelt in 1933.

CONCLUSIONS

The confiscation of gold in 1933 was made possible by structural conditions that no longer exist:

1.) The United States was on a gold standard, which allowed foreign interests to demand gold for dollars if they thought the currency was overvalued.

2.) Gold coins circulated freely as legal tender, and were the primary form of privately-owned gold.

3.) Any public loss of confidence in the dollar or the banking system could lead to a run on gold coins in preference to paper money.

4.) Banks provided a natural enforcement platform for the confiscation of circulating gold coins.

These structural conditions were the basis of the Banking Crisis of 1933, as well as Roosevelt's gold policies, culminating in the Gold Reserve Act of January 30, 1934. They reveal a great deal about the possibility of future gold regulations, including confiscation.

To begin, gold is not nearly as important to our society today as it was in 1933. Neither the value of our money nor the financial well-being of our economy is dependent on the quantity of gold in Fort Knox, and the gold in private hands is completely divorced from the banking system. There is no constitutional interest in privately-held, non-monetary gold, other than property rights. Roosevelt's 10-point statement on the aims and objectives of his gold policies, delivered in 1934, has little application to a modern economy financed with fiat currency.

The structural changes in our monetary and financial systems since 1934 have been so great that they defy any logical reasoning for a second confiscation of gold. The basic motivations for confiscation, as detailed earlier, are inoperative under current conditions. As long as the United States can print money that is both acceptable and useful to other nations, there is no need for gold as international payment. Absolute monetary control cannot be at issue when the Federal Reserve can respond to a financial crisis by creating over $3 trillion out of thin air—as in the case of quantitative easing—to purchase low-quality debt on the books of technically insolvent institutions.

Only monetary restructuring at an international level could influence United States gold policies. I believe this would have to include the remonetization of gold in some form, either as additional backing for current IMF special drawing rights, or as a component for an entirely new world currency. A renewed international recognition of gold as money would lead to mass repatriation of foreign-held dollars, rampant inflation, and an upward spike in the price of gold. These changes would undoubtedly prompt political demands for taxation and regulation of gold. The most important question is whether or not these demands would go as far as confiscation.

In my opinion, the government response to monetizing gold internationally would most likely stop at taxation, coupled with regulation aimed at assisting tax collection. Only in monetary scenario number three, abrupt failure of the dollar, would the government possibly resort to the confiscation of gold, in which case many other individual liberties would also be at risk. Personally, I find it too unlikely and too disturbing to plan for the collapse of society, whereas *increased taxation and regulation are not only likely, but worthy of individual planning.*

Government desire for revenue is far greater than any need to monopolize the domestic gold supply. Various methods of taxing gold, including enhanced enforcement of existing law, mandatory declaration of gold holdings, new taxes on gold sale or transfer, and a one-time capital gains assessment have been previously noted. The most onerous of these would be the so-called "unjustified enrichment" or "windfall profits" tax on capital gains, resulting from international recognition of gold as money. There is no practical or political reason for confiscating physical gold when the primary benefit from ownership—protection from the risks of a depreciating currency—can be taxed as high as 100%. Confiscating an asset yields a one-time benefit; taxing an asset yields an income stream. Steal the eggs, leave the chicken.

Then again, that's just my opinion. I could be wrong.

ACKNOWLEDGMENTS

Credit for this book should rightfully begin with the fraternity of numismatists, both collectors and dealers, who educated me during my 40 years of professional and commercial travel. Although the names are too numerous to list, and some are no longer with us, their sound advice and lasting friendships are not forgotten.

Specific credit for contributions should go to Bob Steinberg, Gary Adkins, and Kirk Menczer for facts and ideas central to my efforts. Unknowing credit also goes to Beth Deisher for inspiring me to address the topic with her *Coin World* editorials. Lastly, I owe my daughter, Jennifer, the greatest thanks for critical assistance with editing and production. Her skill with language is amazing, and her devotion as a daughter is unfailing.

ANNOTATED BIBLIOGRAPHY

One of my lifelong passions has been collecting books on the subject of coins, gold, silver, mining, and sunken treasure, as well as the history of economics, finance, and banking. My library is currently comprised of over 1,400 hardback volumes, in addition to auction catalogs and other coin and precious metal reference manuals. The items listed below were selected for their particular influence on my thinking and this work.

Bloom, Murray Teigh. *Money of their Own.* **New York: Charles Scribner's Sons, 1957.**
A collection of counterfeiting capers, including the story of José Beraha Zdravko, a post-WWII gold coin counterfeiter who defied the British Royal Mint, and won.

Boller, Jr., Paul F. *Presidential Campaigns.* **New York: Oxford University Press, 1984.**
A summary of every presidential campaign from Washington to Reagan, with a 10-page analysis of the 1932 Roosevelt-Hoover contest. For the purposes of this work, the Roosevelt campaign was most notable for what it did not mention concerning the gold standard and the private ownership of gold.

Bordo, Michael D., ED. *The Gold Standard and Related Regimes: Collected Essays.* **Cambridge, United Kingdom: Cambridge University Press, 1999.**
A collection of essays on the history of doctrine and the gold standard, the gold standard as a commodity standard, the gold

standard as a contingent rule, historical case studies, and the Bretton Woods international monetary system.

Bowers, Q. David. *United States Gold Coins: An Illustrated History.* Los Angeles: Bowers and Ruddy Galleries, Inc., 1982.
Most references on this subject offer a date-by-date analysis of each coin type, including die varieties, rarity levels, and market values. Examples include significant numismatic works by Akers, Garret & Guth, and Winter. This book is more general in scope, covering gold discoveries, mining, minting technology, history of collecting, coins as artwork, and legal issues. As a historical reference on U.S. gold coins, it is the most comprehensive single volume, written by the undisputed dean of numismatic literature.

Brooks, John. *Once in Golconda: A True Drama of Wall Street 1920-1938.* New York: W.W. Norton and Co., 1969. Reprint of Harper and Row edition.
A popular history of Wall Street, the Depression, and New Deal finance from 1920 to 1938. Ties together three subjects often treated separately.

Clancy, Kevin. *A History of the Sovereign: Chief Coin of the World.* United Kingdom: Royal Mint Museum Publications, 2015.
An official history of Britain's (and probably the world's) most important gold coin.

Conway, Ed. *The Summit: Bretton Woods, 1944.* New York: Pegasus Books, 2014.
A history of the international financial agreement that brought the world forward from the ashes of World War II. Filled with lively vignettes and colorful characterizations.

Craig, John. *The Mint: A History of the London Mint from A.D. 287 to 1948.* Cambridge, United Kingdom: Cambridge University Press, 1953.
Written by the former Deputy Master and Comptroller of the British Royal Mint, this is the definitive, unsurpassed history of

British minting operations in London from the third to the mid-20th century.

Dam, Kenneth W. *The Rules of the Game: Reform and Evolution in the International Monetary System.* **Chicago: The University of Chicago Press, 1982.**

A history of international monetary agreements, from the gold standard through the collapse of Bretton Woods, followed by a description and analysis of the contemporary system in 1982, and ending with the prospects for reform, including a return to a gold standard. Dated, but historically important.

Dieffenbacher, Alfred. *Counterfeit Gold Coins.* **Montreal, Canada: Dieffenbacher Coin, Ltd., 1963.**

This publication was a counterfeit detection and education service offered to the banks of Canada and Europe in a loose-leaf format to allow for continuous updating. Counterfeit gold coins from France, Germany, Britain, Switzerland, and the U.S. were photographed and enlarged with specific points of detection noted. A standard reference for gold trading windows in Europe, but not widely distributed in the United States since banks didn't trade in gold coins.

Eichengreen, Barry. *Golden Fetters: The Gold Standard and the Great Depression, 1919-1939.* **New York: Oxford University Press, 1992.**

The dictionary defines fetter as anything checking freedom of movement or expression. Professor Eichengreen's thesis is that the gold standard between WWI and the Depression exacerbated the global economic crisis, and constrained positive government response. The style is heavily academic, and emphasizes the role of the gold standard over inadequate political decision-making. The work concludes with analysis of Bretton Woods and events leading to Nixon's abandonment of a gold-backed dollar. Very comprehensive on the history of a gold-backed dollar, but virtually no discussion of confiscation or its necessity.

Einzig, Paul. *The Future of Gold.* **New York: MacMillan and Co., 1935.**

Ibid. Will Gold Depreciate? New York: MacMillan and Co., 1937.

Dr. Einzig wrote a daily column for London's *Financial News* for many years covering the gold standard and international banking. These two works are representative of British and European thinking on the subjects.

Friedman, Milton and Anna Jacobson Schwartz. *A Monetary History of the United States, 1867-1960.* **Princeton, NJ: Princeton University Press, 1963.**

This work was the basis of Professor Friedman's Nobel Prize. The authors make many references to Roosevelt's gold policies, but not in one continuous presentation. Information about confiscation must be extracted and reorganized in order to gain an overall timeline of events. Nonetheless, this book is the best single reference on confiscation I could find, assuming the reader is willing to sift through 800 pages on an intellectual treasure hunt. First editions are highly valuable.

Galbraith, John Kenneth. *Money – Whence It Came, Where It Went.* **Boston: Houghton Mifflin Company, 1975.**

How a distinguished economist can write a 300-page history of money, most of it concerned with events in the United States, and make no mention of Roosevelt's 1933 demand to surrender all privately-held gold coin and gold bullion is difficult to comprehend. Galbraith dislikes gold, and this book reveals his bias. He is a leading proponent of Keynes, and offers an otherwise excellent argument for liberal economics.

Grant, James. *Money of the Mind: Borrowing and Lending in America from the Civil War to Michael Milken.* **New York: Farrar Straus Giroux, 1992.**

Grant is a leading bond expert, and editor of *Grant's Interest Rate Observer.* This book is a history of credit in the United States since the Civil War, from the point of view of a conservative money advocate. One of the few to discuss Roosevelt's policies using the word "confiscation."

Haxby, James A. *Striking Impressions: The Royal Canadian Mint and Canadian Coinage.* **Ottawa, Canada: The Royal Canadian Mint Publications, 1983.**
The official history of the Canadian Mint, including their production of $5, $10, and sovereign gold coins. Canada's gold policies contrasted sharply with U.S. gold policies.

Holzer, Henry Mark. *The Gold Clause: What it is and How to Use it Profitably.* **New York: Books In Focus, 1980.**
This book was published soon after the repeal of Roosevelt's prohibition of gold clauses in contracts, and offers the reader advice on how, when, and why to use a gold clause in modern commerce. Over half the book is devoted to the history of the gold clause, and in particular, the three cases heard simultaneously in 1935 by the Supreme Court before their 5-4 verdict upholding abrogation. It is by far the best historical account of this important ruling that I could find.

Hoppe, Donald J. *How to Invest in Gold Coins.* **New York: Arlington House, 1970.**
Ibid. *How to Invest in Gold Stocks and Avoid the Pitfalls.* **New York: Arlington House, 1972.**
These two books were published about the same time as the closing of the gold window, and a few years before gold ownership was legalized. Both were intended as sound advice on legal avoidance of then-current gold laws, but the titles had the unfortunate ring of get-rich-quick schemes. They are actually well-researched works on the history and economics of gold. The investment advice is woefully outdated, but the history lessons hold true.

Klingaman, William K. *1929: The Year of the Great Crash.* **New York: Harper and Row, 1989.**
This book places the day-by-day financial events of 1929 in context, and views them from multiple perspectives in an unbiased manner. Essential to a comprehensive understanding of the Depression that followed, and more objective than Galbraith's *The Great Crash.*

Kroos, Herman E., ED. *Documentary History of Banking and Currency in the United States, Volumes 1-4.* **New York: Chelsea House Publishers, 1983.**

Hundreds of source documents, including laws, executive orders, and speeches from 1627 to 1968. Most if not all of this information is now available on the internet, but having it in hand is reassuring to this 70-year-old author. An invaluable resource.

Kwarteng, Kwasi. *War and Gold: A 500-Year History of Empires, Adventures, and Debt.* **London: Bloomsbury Publishing, 2014.**

Dr. Kwarteng has a PhD in history from Cambridge University, and served as a member of Parliament. His book surveys the relationship between gold and empire since 1500 A.D., but focuses mainly on the 20th century, portraying Roosevelt's gold policies from a British point of view. He labels the forced sale of gold at $20.67 as "an exercise in expropriation."

Paul, Ron and Lewis Lehrman. *The Case for Gold: A Minority Report of the U.S. Gold Commission.* **Washington D.C.: Cato Institute, 1982.**

A plea for the return to a gold standard from two well-known gold advocates. Named after the committee that officially voted against the measure.

Rickards, James. *Currency Wars: The Making of the Next Global Crisis.* **New York: Portfolio, 2011.**
Ibid. *The Death of Money: The Coming Collapse of the International Monetary System.* **New York: Portfolio, 2014.**
Ibid. *The New Case for Gold.* **New York: Portfolio, 2016.**

The author of these three works has a varied and colorful background, including engagements in intelligence, defense, financial management, and academia. He can be fairly called an alarmist, but his analytic abilities are both brilliant and thought-provoking. Required reading for any student of financial crisis.

Rogoff, Kenneth S. *The Curse of Cash.* **New Jersey: Princeton University Press, 2016.**
Professor Rogoff wants to eliminate all cash in favor of credit cards and electronic payments. He sees cash as evil, facilitating "tax evasion, corruption, terrorism, drug trade, human trafficking, and the rest of a massive global underground economy." When it comes to government control vs. individual freedom, his views are obvious, and may be logically extended to gold as well. He is included here as a representative of opinions that are quite opposite to my own.

Scherman, Harry. *The Promises Men Live By: A New Approach to Economics.* **New York: Random House, 1938.**
The stock market collapse of 1929 and the subsequent Depression of the 1930s created a great deal of doubt in the efficacy of capitalism. Many people looked to government for the top-down, centralized solutions favored by socialism and even Marxism. Harry Scherman's book takes a view of the world from the bottom up, analyzing individual activity in terms of promises made and promises kept. He treats economics as a social and moral construct, rather than a mathematical or mechanical one. His interest is in individual honor and personal reliability, not the speculator's motivations of greed and fear. Had this book been written in 1945, the author might have credited our emergence from economic depression not on the armaments industry, but rather on the social and moral demands of war. Scherman's style is sometimes cumbersome, but his thesis is clear: promises made and promises kept are the bedrock of economic growth and prosperity. A populist response to contemporary Keynesian thinking.

Schilke, Oscar G. and Raphael E. Solomon. *America's Foreign Coins: Foreign Coins with Legal Tender Status in the United States 1793-1857.* **New York: The Coin and Currency Institute, 1964.**
Much more than a catalog of coins, approximately half of this book is devoted to the monetary history and enabling laws behind the nation's dependence on the gold and silver monies of other governments. Readers will be surprised to learn, for ex-

ample, that Spanish escudos and British guineas remained legal tender for 64 years after the first domestic currency in America. A unique reference on the history of gold as money in the United States.

Schlumberger, Hans. *European Gold Coin Guide Book.* **Munich, Germany: Battenberg Verlag, 1975.**
A standard reference for many years that, despite being outdated, is still a source for obscure facts overlooked by modern catalogs.

Stein, Herbert. *The Fiscal Revolution in America.* **Chicago: The University of Chicago Press, 1969.**
Herbert Stein was an advisor to President Roosevelt, and was in the room when many New Deal decisions were made. His work in government continued into the mid-1960s, and his views on government policy are firsthand and objective. He is the consummate insider.

Taber, George M. *Chasing Gold: The Incredible Story of How the Nazis Stole Europe's Bullion.* **New York: Pegasus Books, 2014.**
There are many books on the broad subject of Nazi gold, but none of them are as well-researched as this. Taber follows the trail of gold stored in the central banks of over a dozen countries, from the initial threat of Nazi occupation to the eventual outcome of capture or safe haven. Each case reads like a true-life James Bond adventure. Anyone who doubts the utility of gold as money needs to understand the pivotal role it played in financing World War II.

Taylor, Frederick. *The Downfall of Money: Germany's Hyperinflation and the Destruction of the Middle Class.* **New York: Bloomsbury Press, 2013.**
The destruction of the German economy in 1923 as a result of hyperinflation has been studied endlessly for its political connections to war reparations, the rise of Hitler, anti-Semitism, and World War II. This book focuses instead on the destruction of German society, as the value of the mark plummeted from 300 per dollar to a bottom rate of 4-trillion-to-one. Star-

vation, bankruptcy, institutional collapse, and an intense hatred of the French were only some of the consequences for the average German farmers, shop owners, and retirees in Taylor's book. Today, we laugh at the hyperinflation in Zimbabwe and their paper money with endless zeros. This book reminds us that human misery is not a laughing matter.

United States Treasury Department. *Gold Regulations.* **Washington, D.C.: Government Printing Office, 1961.**
17 pages of fine print legalese, reminding us that Roosevelt's gold policies were still in effect 28 years later, and still based on a national emergency. Required reading for miners, refiners, jewelers, fabricators, importers, exporters, wholesalers, and retailers.

Made in the USA
San Bernardino, CA
12 April 2019